THE CREATION OF THE WEIMAR REPUBLIC

Stillborn Democracy?

PROBLEMS IN EUROPEAN CIVILIZATION

THE CREATION
OF THE WEIMAR REPUBLIC

Stillborn Democracy?

EDITED WITH AN INTRODUCTION BY

Richard N. Hunt

UNIVERSITY OF PITTSBURGH

D. C. HEATH AND COMPANY
A Division of Raytheon Education Company
Lexington, Massachusetts

Table of Contents

Introduction

THE WEIMAR REPUBLIC still evokes strong feelings of sympathy or antipathy in a great many people. Created in 1918 amidst the terrible confusion and bitter despair of Germany's defeat in World War I, it replaced the historic, semi-absolutist regime of the Hohenzollerns with a modern parliamentary democracy. The new government and its supporters were obliged to bear the revenge of the victors embodied in the harsh provisions of the Treaty of Versailles. They also had to struggle against the many enemies of democracy within Germany, from the traditional monarchists on the right to the Communists on the left, and ultimately the Nazis, whose fatal rise to power destroyed the democratic regime in 1933. The fourteen years of the Weimar Republic were fraught with the most violent ideological and national conflicts, conflicts which are still reflected in the historical literature on its creation and its fate.

The Wilhelmian Reich, exhausted by military defeat after four years of total war, came to its end in the spontaneous and largely bloodless November Revolution of 1918. Popular demonstrations in early November aimed at securing immediate peace through the removal of the Kaiser, whose abdication seemed to be demanded by the American president, Woodrow Wilson. After considerable hesitation the Majority Social Democratic Party (SPD), under Friedrich Ebert and Philipp Scheidemann, assumed leadership of the insurgent forces and proclaimed a republic on November 9, signing the armistice that ended the war on November 11. The Social Democrats then sought to maintain order as a caretaker government until a National Assembly could be elected to decide Germany's future. To the left of these moderate socialists were Communists and other radicals who demanded proletarian dictatorship and immediate socialization of the means of production. Threatened by this radical element and not wanting to share the fate of Kerensky in Russia, Ebert allied himself with the Supreme Command of the old army in the person of General Wilhelm Groener. With this military assistance he was able to crush the radicals during scattered fighting early in 1919. The National Assembly, elected in January with a large majority favoring the moderate prorepublican parties, met in Weimar and drew up a constitution that provided Germany with a modern democratic welfare state. But for all its promising features, the Weimar Republic remained weak: its inherited army, civil service, and judiciary served the new state only half-heartedly, and remained essentially authoritarian in spirit and monarchist in loyalty. Dominant elements in the traditional upper classes, their property and position untouched by the Revolution, likewise did not hide their hostility to the new democracy. And, throughout its life, the Republic had to endure the stigma of having been spawned by military defeat and shamed by the dictated Treaty of Versailles. The underlying question raised by the following readings is whether this Republic, Germany's first experiment in democracy, was foredoomed to failure.

All past events rest in a matrix of surrounding historical circumstance. To analyze a single event the historian must cut into this larger matrix, and his perception will depend upon the angle of his dissecting knife. Thus he may cut vertically to perceive the birth of the Weimar Republic as a point in the long stream of German history; he may cut horizontally to see the same event as part of a broader interaction of European and world politics in the early twentieth century; or he may cut out a cross-section to compare with sectional views of other revolutions. These are but three of many methods of analysis — each raises its own questions and produces its own historical controversies.

Some historians see the whole sweep of German history as a straight and irresistible movement toward Nazism. If so, should the creation of the Weimar Republic be regarded as a momentary aberration, brought on by Allied pressure and alien to the German mentality? Or should it, on the other hand, be seen as an important victory for democratic forces whose strength had been growing gradually for half a century within the Second Empire? Would the November Revolution have been more lastingly successful if it had broken less with German tradition, preserving for example the monarchy and perhaps retaining thereby the loyalty and cooperation of the traditional elites? Or could the Revolution have been more successful only by thoroughly destroying the power of these old elites? In practical terms, were either of these options really open to the leaders of the Revolution? To what extent should the choices of 1918–1919 be held responsible for the rise and establishment of Nazism? Nowadays, the Weimar Republic must be related not only to the Nazi experience, but also the experience of the Bonn Republic, which has already surpassed both its immediate predecessors in longevity.

To examine the birth of the Weimar Republic against the longer stream of German history raises many interesting questions, but it ignores the horizontal dimension, the international matrix of the event. Germany's history, because of her geographical location at the center of Europe, has always been particularly intertwined with the history of other countries. The November Revolution itself clearly would not have occurred, had not the Wilhelmian Reich been weakened decisively by four years of total war against the Allied powers. Should the advent of the Republic be regarded as nothing more than the result of Allied pressure, or perhaps even as a deliberate ruse to obtain better peace terms? Or was it a stab in the German back by Social Democrats who selfishly gained power for their own party by selling their fatherland to the enemy? To what extent were German revolutionaries inspired by the Bolshevik example in Russia? Did they receive significant Russian aid? And later, how much of the weakness of the young Republic should be attributed to the harsh provisions of the Versailles Treaty? Did the victorious Allies shortsightedly sabotage German democracy, or was their pressure the only force that kept it in existence at all?

Important questions also arise when one compares the German November Revolution to other revolutions. Should it be considered a revolution at all, or merely the kind of political collapse that seems to occur, under modern conditions, in all countries that suffer defeat in total war? If it was a revolution, where can one find the closest historical parallel: in either of the Russian revolutions of 1917? In the Austrian Revolution of 1918? Or perhaps in the French Revolution of 1870? Communist writers have been particularly troubled in trying to fit the November Revolution into their historical schema. Was it a bourgeois revolution, an abortive proletarian revolution, or something in between? What went wrong to prevent its development in a Communist direction? If it is true, as some historians have argued, that only "revolutions from above" have been successful in Germany, how does one classify the November Revolution? And in terms of a general analysis of political upheaval, do moderate revolutions more often achieve their aims, or radical ones?

In the selections that follow, historians and other writers discuss all of these questions and provide the reader with considerable factual material from which to draw his own conclusions. In the interplay of their conflicting opinions, he may be led to a more mature basis upon which to found his own judgments, and to an interest in the more extensive reading described in the bibliographical essay.

The selections in Part I represent three very sharply contrasting German views of the causes and character of the November Revolution — moderate, right-wing extremist, and left-wing extremist. The distinguished German historian Friedrich Meinecke presents a standard moderate interpretation, which emphasizes the disruptive effects of the war as the primary cause of what followed. The events of November 1918 are seen as a collapse more than as a revolution, an expression of mass disillusion with the war and the old regime. Moreover, he believes that the whole unfortunate train of events might have been avoided if the imperial government had sought an early non-annexationist peace and undertaken domestic reforms. Meinecke's sympathies obviously lie with a democratized constitutional monarchy, which he feels might have survived the war and provided Germany with a stronger, more stable government in the difficult postwar period.

Other writers, both to the right and to the left of Meinecke, reject such an interpretation. Right-wing German nationalists see the November Revolution as a stab in the back (*Dolchstoss*). The crudest and most propagandistic version of the Dolchstoss theory is scarcely worthy of serious consideration on its own historical merits. In the selection chosen, however, the reader may examine a more sophisticated and plausible, semi-scholarly version by Gottfried Zarnow. The writer blames the overthrow of the monarchy on traitorous and self-seeking Social Democratic leaders who handed over their fatherland to the enemy in order to obtain power for themselves. Had Ebert and Scheidemann loyally supported the existing government in early November, internal collapse might have been avoided and an honorable peace obtained for Germany.

Considerations of patriotism and treason naturally do not figure in the Communist accounts of the November Revolution written by East German historians today. Neither do they see a mere collapse, but rather an impressive — although ultimately unsuccessful — effort by the German working class to overthrow the rule of the bourgeoisie. Interestingly enough, this was not always the party line. During the anti-German years of the Stalin period, Communists viewed the Weimar Republic as the creation of a purely bourgeois revolution. But a new wave of younger East German historians, including Roland Bauer, is revising the older interpretation. Bauer discusses the Marxist criteria for analyzing class conflict and concludes that the struggles of 1918–1919 clearly rank as an abortive proletarian revolution, comparable to the Paris Commune of 1871. Unlike the hackneyed phrases ground out by a cynical older generation of Stalinist historians, Bauer's efforts have a ring of earnest sincerity and for this reason, however much the reader may disagree with the views expressed, they deserve serious consideration.

The fateful alliance between the Ebert government and the Supreme Command of the old army, because it seemed to give German militarism a new lease on life, has excited perhaps more historical controversy than any other issue in the November Revolution. Was the alliance a tragic necessity forced upon Ebert by the acute danger of Communist insurrection? Or did Ebert exaggerate the strength of the newly formed German Communist Party (KPD) and neglect the opportunity to create a pro-republican military force, such as the one raised by his fellow Social Democrats in neighboring Austria? A judgment about the Communist threat is obviously involved and the two questions must be treated together. Koppel S. Pinson offers a vigorous defense of Ebert against his many critics, arguing that the unfortunate alliance was made necessary by the dangerous Communist policy of fomenting violence and civil war. He feels that the KPD should therefore bear the blame for the revival of German militarism, while Ebert deserves praise for having saved Germany from chaos and Bolshevism.

A much different assessment of Communist strength and tactics emerges from the remarkably detached analysis of Eric Waldman. This American political scientist contends that the KPD had neither the capability nor the intention of carrying out a second revolution in the first critical months of the Weimar Republic. In harmony with this interpretation are the conclusions of S. William Halperin, a liberal American historian of the Weimar Republic, who censures the Social Democratic leaders severely for failing to create a republican army, even after this policy was prescribed for them by the National Congress of Councils. He believes that Ebert's alliance with the Supreme Command crippled the Republic from the outset by giving anti-democratic elements a monopoly of military power.

The debate over Social Democratic military policy fits into a broader debate over the possible existence of a "Third Way." Looking back from the failure of the Republic, many writers have wondered whether there might not have been some third alternative avenue of development for the November Revolution, between Communist dictatorship on the one hand, and the tragic compromises of the Weimar Republic on the other. Those who perceive such an avenue not only sympathize with the proposed creation of a republican army, but also look with favor on the council movement and the demands for social and economic reform, especially those for the break-up of the Junker estates and the socialization of heavy industry. The classic exponent of this view was the German left-wing socialist historian, Arthur Rosen-

berg, whose early writings on the birth of the Weimar Republic were widely influential. Many American historians, who did not necessarily share Rosenberg's socialist opinions, accepted his arguments for social and economic reform as a safeguard for political democracy. Only through such reform, it is contended, could the power of the anti-democratic upper classes in Germany have been broken, and the social foundation for a stable democracy laid down. The failure to undertake such a program made it possible for these reactionary elements, their power intact, to sabotage and eventually help destroy the Weimar Republic in concert with Adolf Hitler.

Critics of the Third Way have replied, like Pinson in regard to military questions, that the responsible Social Democratic leaders had no choice but to follow the policies they did. In the social and economic sphere no less than in the military, their freedom of action was drastically curtailed by the most urgent necessities. Former Social Democratic parliamentary leader, Hermann Müller, defends his party's economic policies in the revolutionary period, arguing that the exhausted condition of the economy, after four years of war, precluded immediate socialization, while the critical food shortage made experiments in land reform unfeasible.

The polemics of Rosenberg and Müller belong to the interwar years; a younger generation of scholars has tackled the same questions with an additional quarter-century of historical perspective. Klaus Epstein, a German-born American historian, has come to the defense of the Weimar Social Democrats against those Rosenberg-influenced American writers who have blamed them for the failures of the Revolution. Evaluating the prewar development of the SPD, Epstein sees in the growth of Bernstein's reformism the best hope of party success in the admittedly adverse climate of Wilhelmian Germany. That this reformism failed in 1918 to create a stable and lasting democracy should not be blamed on the ideology, or on the leaders who accepted it, but on the unfavorable German environment and the impossibly difficult circumstances of the time. There simply was no Third Way in the November Revolution.

On the other side, the young German historian Peter von Oertzen gives new vigor to the Rosenberg interpretation by a close examination of the Ruhr miners' movement in the revolutionary period. He presents evidence for the existence of a broad Third Way consensus among the mass of Ruhr miners who, transcending the doctrinal divisions among the socialist parties, aimed at socialization of the mines under genuinely democratic council control. Had the SPD government leaders supported — rather than suppressed — this and similar movements, he feels that an economically feasible socialization could have been effected which would have dispossessed the reactionary industrialists and eclipsed the Communists at the same time.

The fate of the young Weimar Republic depended not only upon the constellation of internal forces that supported and opposed it, but also upon the attitudes and policies of the victorious Allied powers. Did the stringently enforced paragraphs of the Versailles Treaty hamstring the Republic from the beginning? From the bitter perspective of 1933, many German republicans certainly thought so. The shortsighted vindictiveness of the Allies, it seemed to them, had placed an impossible burden on the fragile new democracy, punishing the wrong Germans and rekindling the very fires of militarism and extreme nationalism that the visitors had fought to suppress. In the wake of an even harsher defeat in 1945, Golo Mann, a gifted German historian, modifies somewhat the earlier German judgments of Versailles. With considerable sophistication Mann treats the complicated national passions — German and non-German alike — that affected the treaty writing, but concludes that Versailles did indeed harm the Republic by poisoning its relations with the outside world, and by giving aid and comfort to the domestic enemies of democracy.

Diametrically opposite are the conclusions of the widely read British historian A. J. P. Taylor. Writing in a particularly Germanophobic mood at the close of World War II, Taylor denies that German democracy was injured by the treaty. On the contrary, he states, democratic institutions were created in Germany only because of Allied pressure and remained in existence only as long as that pressure continued. While Germany richly deserved the Treaty of Versailles, the causes of republican failure must be sought elsewhere. Taylor finds them in the general weakness of democratic forces within Germany and in the virulent nationalism which infected all Germans, even the well-meaning but ineffectual Social Democrats.

In Part V a German political scientist, Theodor Eschenburg, integrates the several aspects of the historical problem, national and international, in a trenchant analysis. Emphasizing the "improvised" and incomplete character of Germany's democratization, he stresses the continuity of the authoritarian institutions and forces that survived the upheaval: the army, the civil service, the judiciary, the educational system, the Lutheran Church, the East-Elbian latifundia, and heavy industry. All these remained to undermine the promising democratic forms of the Weimar Republic. It is left to the reader to decide, in the last analysis, whether this Republic ever had a chance or whether it was doomed from the outset.

The Conflict of Opinion

"A voluntary and timely abdication by the Emperor and his equally burdened heir would not only have precluded the insolent demand of the enemy but perhaps the threatening revolution as well."

—— FRIEDRICH MEINECKE

"The internal enemies of Germany, won over by the foe, used an opportune moment to stab us in the back. . . ."

—— GOTTFRIED ZARNOW

"The November Revolution . . . was the first attempt of the German proletariat to seize state power and to establish the political dominion of the working class."

—— ROLAND BAUER

"The Spartacist tactics of revolt was a policy of catastrophe which drove the Majority Socialists into the arms of the reactionary militarists. . . ."

—— KOPPEL S. PINSON

"In spite of the Spartacists' violent opposition to any action directed toward a consolidation of the unfinished revolution, they did not plan, prepare, or organize an armed uprising with the intention of overthrowing the government. . . ."

—— ERIC WALDMAN

"The Representatives of the People did not touch the property either of the east Elbian landowners or of the coal magnates in the Ruhr district. A positive economic policy in the direction of Socialism would nevertheless have been possible. . . ."

—— ARTHUR ROSENBERG

"It is true that Ebert refused to create a socialist *fait accompli*. . . . The bloodshed, chaos, and famine resulting from such a policy (whether successful or not) would have provided an even worse foundation for the creation of German democracy than that upon which Weimar was actually built."

—— KLAUS EPSTEIN

"The peace treaty affected Germany in two ways. It created a distorted, unnatural relationship between Germany and the world, its neighbors to the

West and the East; and it divided the nation because one group of politicians and their supporters quickly found themselves insidiously being made to shoulder the responsibility for every misfortune."

—— Golo Mann

"From start to finish the German republic, and the entire structure of German democracy, owed its existence to the supremacy of Allied arms."

—— A. J. P. Taylor

I. THE CAUSES AND CHARACTER OF THE NOVEMBER REVOLUTION

Unfortunate Collapse—A Liberal View

FRIEDRICH MEINECKE

Perhaps the most renowned of recent German historians is Friedrich Meinecke, whose long life encompassed the entire century between Bismarck and Adenauer. From a conservative background, and trained in the nationalist school of German historiography, Meinecke migrated politically to the left liberal (Progressive) camp in the years prior to World War I. Although he subsequently became a loyal supporter of the Weimar Republic (and was silenced during the Hitler period), the essay below—written in 1930—expressed a kind of nostalgic and patriotic regret that the constitutional monarchy was not able to democratize itself in time to prevent the November Revolution. His masterful historical analysis receives an added degree of authenticity because he was personally acquainted with the principal actors and witnessed many of the events he describes.

EVERY MODERN WAR is a test of endurance for the existing governmental order. It was, however, especially difficult in the World War for those nations which still had an authoritarian monarchy. In 1887 Bismarck told the Czar with deep conviction that the interest of the great monarchies today more than in any other historical epoch demanded that wars be avoided. He pursued after 1871 a policy of world peace, but was armed for war and, for that very reason, remained equally capable of conducting a firm peace policy or a strong control in the war, if it were unavoidable. He rejected parliamentarism and held fast to a strong constitutional monarchy. Therefore he created a domestic political system that would be independent of the fluctuations of political parties. But this system required unusually strong and insightful national leaders in order to maintain itself against the domestic social forces. And it had the disadvantage of not offering enough outlets for these forces. To be sure, the social forces already matured at the time of the establishment of the Empire were satisfied by Bismarck's system. It depended upon the cartel of the aristocratic conservative strata ruling previously in old Prussia with the German liberal middle class, and could gradually incorporate, after the end of the *Kulturkampf*, the Catholic population of Germany, represented by the Center Party. The middle classes were won over to Bismarck's system by his great national achievements, which also stimulated eco-

From Friedrich Meinecke, "Die Revolution, Ursachen und Tatsachen," *Handbuch des Deutschen Staatsrechts,* ed. Gerhard Anschütz and Richard Thoma (Tübingen, 1930), Vol. I, pp. 95–112. Reprinted by permission of Verlag J. C. B. Mohr (Paul Siebeck).

[In this and the following articles the footnote documentation has been omitted. All translations are by the editor.]

nomic life, and by the security it gave them from the revolutionary goals of the newly rising Social Democratic proletariat. But this movement, with its swelling masses, remained outside the system, hostile to the existing state and treated hostilely by it. Quietly, there occurred even here a gradual rapprochement to the old state, because of the effects of the state's social welfare program, because of the influx into the party of elements that were dissatisfied but not revolutionary, and because of the slow conversion of revolutionary socialist ideals into evolutionary ones. But the foundation of state power, the army, was weakened — compared to the era of unification — by the social effects of economic development during the last half-century, for which the Bismarckian system was not adapted. Was it still possible, without risking political collapse in case of defeat, to conduct a great war in the spirit of national solidarity, with complete utilization of compulsory military service, when the pro-state disposition which compulsory military service presupposes no longer or only insufficiently existed in a large part of the nation?

Equally unsatisfactory was the other presupposition of the Bismarckian system, the personality of the ruler, who either himself or through suitable selection of the chancellor had to perform the functions of an authoritarian constitutional monarch. William II's confidence in his own political capability (a confidence which had long since disappeared among the experts) suffered a decisive blow through the Daily Telegraph Affair of 1908. With this began the great historical process which was to lead to the collapse of the monarchy. The last chancellor he chose before the war was a tragic personality, comparable to the older Radowitz, advisor of Friedrich William IV, who recognized the great needs of national life and began to fulfill them, but was prevented from doing so completely by internal and external disruptions. Bethmann-Hollweg knew, when the war broke out in 1914, what was at stake for Germany and especially for the monarchy in the event of defeat. To fight through this battle for existence with the old system unchanged seemed to him impossible, and rightly so. Thus there ensued the second act in the transformation of the old system: the reception of Social Democracy among the parties supporting the state. The arrest of Social Democratic leaders envisaged in the mobilization plan was not carried out. The Emperor set the theme in the decisive August days of 1914: "I no longer recognize any parties, I recognize only Germans."

That might have seemed the splendid beginning of a new era of the constitutional monarchy, resting on an extended popular foundation. But now the third moment of transformation arrived. The Emperor declined to follow the strong words of his earlier years with strong deeds. He did not feel equal to the gigantic burden which the war thrust upon him. He let his subordinates command and rule. But therewith disappeared that single unifying force which constitutional monarchy presupposes. In the highest position of state a vacuum set in, which could be tolerated for a time, but which in a severe crisis had to lead to a usurpation of power from the other side, and to a further transformation of the system. Confidence in the cooperation of the working masses, to be sure, proved at first to be justified. The Social Democratic Reichstag fraction decided among themselves on August 3, by 78 votes to 14, to favor war credits, and then voted for them unanimously (because of party discipline) on August 4. According to the doctrine of the party the class struggle and the international solidarity of the proletariat ranked supreme, and the socialists of all countries should oppose the outbreak of a war with all their strength (Stuttgart Convention of the International, 1907). Even in the last days of July, as Europe headed toward war, the Party acted according to these principles and sought contact with the French socialists (Hermann Müller's mission to Paris). But even Bebel had always acknowledged the duty to defend one's country against attack, and the Russian mobilization gave to the beginning of the war a defensive character, while the struggle against reactionary Russia also corresponded to socialist ideology. To refuse war credits would have meant not only to paralyze the defensive power of the nation, but also to expose the party to severe persecution and internal crisis. Tactical considerations of a binding nature and an overriding burst of patriotism worked together in the epoch-making vote of August 4. The small group of those who had dissented on August 3 (among others the party chairman Haase, Ledebour, and Liebknecht) remained on the horizon as portents of new storms to come.

Two things had to happen in order to maintain national unity and protect the monarchical state from the danger of overthrow in case of defeat. The principle had to be observed that Germany would conduct a defensive war, and would not prolong the conflict for the sake of imperialistic goals of conquest. And it was necessary to undertake the promised "New Orientation" in domestic policy (expression of Minister Clemens von Delbrück, March 10, 1915) to satisfy the desires of the working class for a full equality of political rights and for greater political influence. Both requirements, however, were obstructed by those parties and strata which supported the Bismarckian system domestically. The early victories of German arms awakened in them demands for expansion, above all at the expense of Belgium, demands which were motivated by the desire to provide Germany with better protection from future attacks, but which also were nourished by the consideration that only a manifest victory could secure the conservative-aristocratic and upper middle-class system of government domestically. Their annexationism broke one of the main clauses of the silent contract which Social Democracy had concluded with the state and the other parties for the salvation of the fatherland. Indeed a naive annexationism was also widespread in the lower strata of the nation and in the fighting forces, as long as things went well

on the battlefield or seemed to go well. But when the number of enemies grew, the horrible effects of the starvation blockade set in, and no end of the war was in sight, these faint desires for expansion waned among the masses, and the hardening annexationism of the upper strata was felt by them as the greatest obstacle to peace. It split the nation and weakened the will of the home front to fight. The Reichstag Peace Resolution of July 19, 1917 was supposed to banish the masses' concern that the war would be prolonged for the sake of annexationist goals. But the uncertain attitude of the government toward it (Michaelis' words, "as I interpret it," July 19), the absence of an official declaration on the return of Belgium, and the new proof of annexationistic policies at the peace negotiations of Brest-Litovsk early in 1918, aroused the masses once more. The big January strike of 1918 in Berlin (beginning January 28) had other causes as well, but was conceived by its leaders as an answer to the so-called Hoffmann Punch at Brest-Litovsk (January 12).

The second clause of the unwritten contract between Social Democracy and the state was the carrying out of the New Orientation. The most pressing demand was the reform of the Prussian three-class system of voting, which gave clearest expression to the second-class citizenship of the proletariat, and which therefore formed not only politically but also psychologically the greatest barrier between the working class and the state. The idea seemed intolerable that the war profiteer, who had feathered his nest by odious means, was to have incomparably more electoral weight than the returning poor front-soldier. It is true that the soldier in the field did not speak much about electoral reform. Probably more pressing things were on his mind. But for the home front which had to provide the source of strength for the fighting forces, the unsolved question of electoral reform became one of the seeds of discontent, which appeared more and more clearly after 1916, after the unsuccessful assaults on

Verdun. The Russian Revolution of March 1917 also exerted an enormous influence. One of its first acts was the proclamation of a general, equal, and secret franchise (by Prince Lvov). A wave of strikes, which broke out in April 1917 in Berlin and other industrial cities and which was evoked directly by the famine of the "turnip winter," served as a warning to the government that, if it could not give the people bread, it should give them political rights. Bethmann was indeed long since convinced of the necessity of electoral reform, but felt too weak to carry it through in one stroke against the opposing conservative forces, and so tried instead to loosen the crust gradually. The Easter message of the Emperor (April 7, 1917) held out the definite prospect of an electoral reform after the war that would eliminate the class system of voting, and create a direct and secret, but still not equal, franchise. When famine and unrest grew, and the failure of unrestricted submarine warfare evoked a deep depression in the Reichstag (speech of Erzberger, July 6, 1917), Bethmann put through on July 11, 1917, one day before his fall, a cabinet order which promised an equal franchise and ordered the reform pushed forward without delay. But the bill introduced by the government in December 1917 provoked a resistance among the Prussian Conservatives that could not be restrained. Thus dissolved the possibility of reconciling, by a great liberal gesture, the privileged segment of the population and the alienated one. When the Prussian House of Lords on October 24, 1918 finally accepted the equal franchise, it was too late to check the development toward revolution.

One should not, however, see the causes of the revolution exclusively in the failures of the government and the ruling classes. To win the entire Social Democratic proletariat over to the state by means of reforms was precluded from the outset, because the Marxist ideology of class struggle and the international solidarity of the proletariat was so deeply rooted in a smaller section of the party that it rejected all thought of rapprochement with the old order. Even here, a victory of the capitalistic Entente powers was not desired, but neither was a crushing victory for German arms, because of the fear that from it would result a powerful strengthening of the reactionary system. In these quarters there was more indifference toward the duty of national defense and a more hostile disposition toward the old state than in the predominating mass of the Party and in the largest part of the trade unions, which were resolved to carry all the burdens of the war in exemplary fashion. The announcement of victories by the Supreme Command and the expansion of German arms into enemy territory gave the minority the argument that the goal of German security had been attained, and that therefore one could and must now undertake more radical agitation in domestic matters.

The first one from the Social Democratic Reichstag fraction who dared break party discipline and vote against war credits was Karl Liebknecht on December 2, 1914. At the next session concerning credits, on March 20, 1915, 30 members of the Party left the hall before the voting, and 2 voted against. On December 29, 1915, of 43 opposition fraction members, 20 now followed the example of Liebknecht by a public rejection of credits. First Liebknecht and Rühle, and then on March 24, 1916 the remaining 18, were expelled from the fraction (though not yet the Party), and now formed a Reichstag fraction of their own. Some of its representatives at the Kienthal Conference of the International (April 1916), the group around Ledebour, associated themselves with the resolution to fight against the continuance of the war with all — even revolutionary — means. Still more radical, however, was the group led by Liebknecht and Rosa Luxemburg which in 1916 created for their revolutionary agitation the medium of the Spartacus Letters. An extreme left formed in Bremen under Radek. The framework of the old Party, under these divisions, was bound to rupture.

On January 16, 1917 the leaders of the Party majority carried out the separation, and on April 6, 1917 there followed in Gotha — under the impression of the Russian Revolution — the establishment of the Independent Social Democratic Party of Germany (USPD), henceforth against the Majority Socialists (MSPD). Several of the Independents had a hand in calling out the April strike of 1917.

The USPD was not — and did not become — a closed revolutionary party, but concealed within itself very diverse shadings of opinion, as is usually the case with radicalizations on the eve of a possible but not yet definite revolution. All of them probably wished that the end of the war might lead to a forceful overthrow of the old system, but the group furthest to the right under Haase and Dittmann was careful in assessing the chances and in their choice of tactical methods. The group around Ledebour was stormier, while the little Spartacus group under Liebknecht and Rosa Luxemburg was even more ready for revolution — in the spirit of the Russian Bolsheviks — and remained under the protective roof of the USPD organization, although ideologically separated from it by a consistent determination to set up a dictatorship of the proletariat. It depended on the course of the war whether the illegal agitation that the USPD and Spartacus, carried on by means of leaflets, confidential agents, etc., would obtain significant results in the country and in the army. Their most effective weapon was the cry for peace, for a peace without annexations or indemnities, which the masses might obtain by force of their pressure — and which could then among irresponsible elements easily turn into the cry for peace at any price.

Majority Socialists, Independents, and Left Radicals struggled henceforth for the minds of the workers. The Majority Socialists could not retain their supporters by the appeal to a sense of patriotic duty alone. They were in the most difficult historical situation imaginable for a political party. Since the beginning of the war, they were also among themselves in the process of a "New Orientation" and transformation of old ideals and concepts, all of which was not possible without certain individual incongruities. They could not abandon the mass basis which gave them power — but this mass was now politically unsettled. To demand from them in each of their acts the composure of an experienced government party was unfair. As an emerging government party, the Social Democrats achieved the utmost possible for them by their strict adherence to the idea of national defense, and one could not expect them to ignore the growing discontent. Insofar as they expressed that discontent, no doubt, they abetted it as well. Only tangible successes for their newly oriented pro-government policies, such as the granting of electoral reform and the clear restriction of war aims to simple defense, could have improved their position with respect to the masses, and could have softened their language toward the ruling classes. But these successes were lacking.

Three events in the first months of the year 1917 hastened by their concurrence the sinister development of revolution: the winter famine, the unrestricted submarine war, and the Russian Revolution. Food supplies sank to a low level, which could no longer be raised substantially by the somewhat better harvests of the following years, and which provided on the average only 1400 calories instead of the normal 3000 for the daily ration of the individual. The waiting in line in front of food stores made the exhausted people unruly and rebellious, and above all furious at the rich who secretly fed themselves better. The moral bonds of society gave way.

The decision of January 9, 1917 for unrestricted submarine warfare, extorted by the Supreme Command from the reluctant chancellor Bethmann, was a further act in the already begun transformation of the Bismarckian system, one which can be designated either as a corruption or as an exaggeration. It was a corruption in that the primacy of the political leadership over the military, so strictly preserved by Bismarck, was broken. It was an exaggeration in that the military element of the old Prussian system stepped over its limits. And at the same time it was also for the nation a symptom of the disappearing confidence in victory among the ruling circles and of the exhaustion of our normal methods of combat, that this desperate step was ventured which would have to bring America into the war. If the venture had been successful, there would have been general rejoicing. But on July 6 Erzberger, in the main committee of the Reichstag, could give that frightening speech which buried hope for any conceivable success. The decision for unrestricted submarine warfare, thus I was told a year later by Bethmann himself, was our Sicilian expedition; that is, it resembled the adventure of Alcibiades which led Athens into the abyss.

The Russian Revolution, finally, provided an example of how a powerful administrative and military structure, extended over the masses, could suddenly collapse because faith in the system had been shaken by failure in arms. Militarily it was a stroke of luck for us, but politically it weakened the authority of our own system of government and increased the expectation, whether anxious or hopeful, that a revolution might also be forthcoming for us.

During the July Crisis of 1917 internal tensions exploded for the first time. How it involved the problems of annexationism and electoral reform we have already discussed. Even more important were the shocks in internal structure which it produced for the whole life of the state. The Bismarckian system, a system of constitutional monarchy which presupposed strong, statesmanlike leadership in all branches of government, now came apart at the seams, and on the horizon appeared two possible replacements: a parliamentary democratic system, supported by the left-wing parties and the masses, or a military dictatorship, supported by heavy industry and the nationalistic upper classes. The proponents of these alternate systems clashed with one another, and their opposition still has its effects today.

The course of events can only be summarized here. The critical war situation was combined with the inadequacy of those who represented the old system. It is of extreme dramatic moment that the Emperor and Chancellor found themselves together on July 11 in granting the equal franchise, attempting therewith to take up once again the direction of events — and then on the next day came Hindenburg and Ludendorff's threat of resignation, which demanded the dismissal of Bethmann as a condition for their remaining. They saw in him the pernicious weakling, who stood in the way of the complete mobilization of national energies. They themselves, however, were indispensable, not only because of their accomplishments, but also because of the almost blind confidence which they enjoyed among the people. The Emperor did not feel strong enough to put them back in their places, to command them to remain while he held onto Bethmann. Bethmann, whose authority in the previous days had also decreased in the Reichstag, now reaped the fruit of his policies. Indeed, he wanted what was right and strove for it, but — out of an excessive fatalism — did not dare to lead the fight for primacy on a large scale. The Supreme Command, which brought about his fall, now entered into national life as a completely new, revolutionary factor, which was not at all provided for in the constitution. Two precedent-setting instances of their own successful intervention were now at hand: unrestricted submarine warfare and the fall of Bethmann. The Emperor had become a shadow monarch.

This action of the Supreme Command became linked with simultaneous actions in the Reichstag which, in the most peculiar and contradictory manner, and by strange combination with various intrigues, promoted the goal of the Supreme Command and the Right to overthrow Bethmann. But in the final analysis this action gravitated toward the goal they hated: the parliamentarization of the Reich constitution.

Now suddenly in the confusion that had arisen through Erzberger's disclosure of July 6, the idea emerged among the Majority Social Democrats — and not only among them — to realize the old ideal of parliamentary government through the new men who were called to leadership. It is historically invalid to dismiss this new demand as a mere yearning for power and an attempt to exploit an unfortunate situation. It arose now not only because confidence in a victorious peace was lost, but even the hope that the existing government could attain a conciliatory peace. For the first time, the majority was formed out of the Center, Left Liberals, and Majority Social Democrats, whose historical task it would later become to erect anew and remold the shaken state. This majority had already passed the Peace Resolution of July 19, mentioned in another connection, and extracted from the new government of Chancellor Michaelis a kind of recognition, albeit with reservations. It has been argued (by Bredt) that if only it had had the necessary determination, it could have carried through the parliamentarization of the Reich constitution and directed developments into more favorable channels that would have made the revolution unnecessary. But left-wing deputies of that time have rightly objected that it was necessary to postpone the attack against the old forces. Our wartime unity, they say, hindered us. A struggle by parliament for complete power would have produced a counter-thrust by the military dictatorship, and therewith an insuperable crisis. The Supreme Command appeared to the Reichstag, as it did to the monarch, as the more powerful political factor.

And it remained such as long as it was indispensable, even when it no longer seemed to offer the certainty of victory, but only a possibility. That was the secret of its power. The new pressures of its opponent, the Reichstag Majority, continued, but their accomplishments (the appointment of parliamentarians as secretaries of state, etc.; prior consultation of the parties

before the appointment of Hertling as chancellor on November 1, 1917) receded before the weight of the decisions which were taken by the Supreme Command. The Eastern peace treaties of Brest-Litovsk (March 3, 1918) and Bucharest (May 7, 1918) made it possible for the Supreme Command to venture a great offensive once again in France for the purpose of attaining a victorious peace also in the West — the last and highest climax of its political desire, which was seconded enthusiastically by the right-wing strata now organized in the Fatherland Party (founded September 2, 1917 in protest against the Peace Resolution). All the social forces and ideas included in Bismarck's system were united here: the landed aristocracy, the officer corps, the propertied and educated bourgeoisie, with their capitalistic interests as well as their national and nationalistic ideals. But the unifying bond of this Bismarckian system, the strong political leadership of a monarch or a statesman, was severed. That was the tragic situation in which the Bismarckian world went toward the final showdown. It had scorned the road to a conciliatory peace. It is indeed doubtful whether such was attainable, given the disposition of the Entente after America's entry made it overwhelmingly powerful. But at least looking for a way would have had good effects domestically and diminished the tension between right and left. Now during the great spring offensive of 1918 the energies of the leftist camp were again directed toward the war, for the fate of the fatherland was at stake, and only the relatively few elements which wanted revolution did not share the strong desires of the rest for victory. But when the bow of our power, stretched to the utmost, burst instead of letting loose the fatal arrow, the consequences were not to be predicted.

Shortly before the breakdown of the last offensive (July 15 and 18, 1918) the dictatorship of the Supreme Command won another domestic political victory. State secretary von Kuhlmann, the spokesman of a conciliatory peace, was dismissed at its urging. On the evening before his dismissal (July 8), the author was with him and heard from him the sombre words: "Revolutions arise from the mistakes of foreign policy. If the classes called upon to lead the nation do not understand their mission and do not know how to find the way to peace, they lose their authority over the masses and the whole thing breaks to pieces."

The starvation blockade helped in breaking down resistance, both physically and morally. Physically it probably hit the lower urban strata more heavily than the upper. Its moral effect was also different in the various sections of the nation and the army. The upper strata, which were more closely bound to the state, maintained a firmer attitude. This was apparent even among those individuals who suffered physically as much as the lower strata, and shows how crucially important in modern war is the cohesion between the individual and the state. Next, the front army held out better than the home army. The atmosphere of real war hardened the men. This was evident in the case of the navy. The crews of submarines did their duty to the end. But the non-engagement of the large battleships had a devastating effect on the mind. The best officers and crews were pulled off them for submarine duty; the youngest and oldest remained, sometimes sailors who already had served six or seven years, and who now had to perform day-in, day-out painstaking service on those large dark iron vessels, work necessary to keep them busy and disciplined. But this leaden life was hard to take over a long period. They began to rebel internally against the yoke, complained bitterly about degrading treatment from the officers and inadequate care, gathered together those of similar opinions and turned their eyes to that party which seemed to work most radically for immediate peace, the Independents. That this party itself incited to mutiny has not been proved. But it did not deny the accusations, and it gave the sailors propaganda material and rejoiced when they came over to the Party in throngs. A revolutionary mood was arising and the Russian model haunted everyone's mind. When in July and August 1917 things became acute through various acts of crass rebellion, the authorities intervened sharply and restored external peace by carrying out two death sentences. But hardly anything was changed in the essential conditions on the ships.

Driven by the ardent desire to obtain peace forcibly in the great spring offensive of 1918, the front army exerted itself beyond belief. But from the moment when the failure of the offensive was known — the middle of July — signs of slackening and disintegration set in. They were visible less among the experienced troops, who fought on with indescribable exertion, than among the replacements who inadequately filled the thinning ranks, and who proved to a large degree undisciplined and afraid of war. As a punishment, the leaders of the great January strike had thoughtlessly been sent to the front, where they now propagandized disastrously. And the troops brought from the East had already experienced the influences of Bolshevism.

During the period from July 18 through November 11, the German army in the West lost in dead and wounded about 420,000 men, in prisoners and missing about 340,000. Masses of deserters grouped together behind the front. The phrases, "strikebreaker" and "prolonger of the war," were first shouted in August at advancing troops. During the course of the war years the relationship of the officers to the men had deteriorated. The remains of the active officer corps, with which the army had marched off in 1914, had been pulled back for staff duty. The active officer had received a higher measure of respect and confidence from the men than the young reserve lieutenant taking his place, who was trained quickly and made an officer according to somewhat external criteria, and who usually did not have the proper tact in the treatment of soldiers who often were twice as old as he was. The traditional gap between officers and men, which expressed itself in the sharp difference between the lieutenant's pay and the soldier's, was now especially hard to bear. Also, an historically significant change in the structure of the old corps took place in the course of the war. This new militia officer corps, which from a military viewpoint still achieved a great deal, resembled politically and socially a weaker beam that had to be put in place of a stronger one which had been destroyed. One must always bear in mind that these defects in the army began to shake the originally powerful authority of the old regime only when the hope for final victory was broken. They belong, therefore, to the secondary causes of the revolution.

By September 29, things had gone so far that the Supreme Command had to demand the immediate opening of truce and peace negotiations. The military situation indeed improved somewhat in the next few days and weeks, but it was only a matter of time before the great preponderance given the Entente by America's entry would put the exhausted and poorly equipped German army out of action. The war reports which had fostered dangerous illusions in the previous years now had to reveal the seriousness of the situation. The announcement of September 29 hit the masses like a thunderclap, not to mention the strata still living deep in illusions. Belief in the maintenance of the old regime received a decisive blow. The power of action, out of an inner necessity, devolved upon those who had represented the ideas of a conciliatory peace and domestic reform, the inevitable democratization of the political system. It was not decisive that the Entente, to encourage internal dissention, had demanded the democratization of Germany, but rather that the national catastrophe now demanded the highest degree of cohesion between the state and the people. The bond missing in the Bismarckian constitution now had to be produced on the spur of the moment: the Majority Social Democrats had to enter the government. Even before the armistice demands, in the darkening situation, this thought had been grasped. On September 30 the Emperor declared, in

accepting the resignation of Chancellor Hertling, "I desire that the German people cooperate more actively than hitherto in determining the fate of the fatherland. It is consequently my will that men who have the confidence of the people participate to a great extent in the rights and duties of government." On October 3 Prince Max of Baden, the humane representative of a peace based on justice, was appointed chancellor. He sprang immediately into the breach in order to save the monarchy.

But it could only be saved as a parliamentarized monarchy. It might have been conceivable to seek transitional forms between the existing constitutional monarchy, which entrusted the choice of ministers to the monarch, and a parliamentary monarchy which binds the monarch in the choice of ministers to the wishes of a parliamentary majority. Such a transitional form had been tried in the appointment of Hertling. Now Count Roedern suggested another transitional form which would include representatives not only of the majority parties, but of all the large parties in a cabinet of national unity. At the beginning of the war this solution would have been feasible; now it was too late. The right-wing parties were too heavily burdened by their stands against a conciliatory peace and electoral reform for the left-wing parties now to share responsibility with them. The new "war cabinet" was thus formed from the majority that had passed the Peace Resolution.

The existing Bismarckian constitution of the Reich now had to be transformed in order to give free reign to a parliamentary regime. It was only tragic that the constitutional change no longer appeared as the pure expression of the autonomous will of the majority, with the assent of the monarch, but now had to occur as the dictate of the enemy. The second Wilson note, issued October 14 in response to our armistice request of October 3, demanded either the destruction of the hitherto existing imperial power or at least its reduction to practical impotence. On October 26 the

Reichstag passed the constitutional changes that effected this impotence, and on October 28 the Emperor promulgated them. In the future the consent of the Reichstag was to be necessary for the declaration of war and the making of peace treaties; the chancellor needed the confidence of the Reichstag; the appointment of officers required the counter-signature of the chancellor or the minister of war, etc. At the same time the main force behind the military quasi-government (which had rocked the Bismarckian system for almost two years) fell when Ludendorff was dismissed on October 26 and replaced by the liberal and socially minded General Groener.

In the meantime a still stronger and more humiliating blow was dealt by the enemy — so strong and so weighty that it must be reckoned among the most important causes of the revolution. The third Wilson note of October 23, not satisfied with the changes already projected in the constitution, declared that if one had to deal with the military rulers and monarchical autocrats of Germany, one must not conduct peace negotiations but demand surrender. That was equivalent to demanding the abdication of the Emperor. The thought of it was already in the air. In the first half of September, thinking statesmen had made clear, as the author can testify, that the monarchy could only be saved in this catastrophe by the creation of a regency, and that the Entente would not negotiate with the Emperor. It appeared psychologically impossible that the inevitable parliamentary monarchy could be viable under an Emperor with such a past. A voluntary and timely abdication by the Emperor and his equally burdened heir would not only have precluded the insolent demand of the enemy but perhaps the threatening revolution as well. Now, after the third Wilson note, even the Bavarian government on October 25 suggested that the Emperor should make the painful sacrifice. What seemed to speak against it was the concern that the abdication of the Supreme Commander would have a devastating effect

upon the overtired front army, so that it would, as Hindenburg expressed it, disperse like a band of marauders. The behavior of the army after the ninth of November, and in the withdrawal, does not testify that this would have happened. The Emperor avoided the anticipated demands for abdication by his sudden departure to the main headquarters at Spa on October 29. But on the same evening the Social Democratic state secretary Scheidemann declared to Prince Max that for the Emperor to remain in office would worsen the prospects for a tolerable armistice and peace. Thus the hope of the October days, the attempt to transform the old authoritarian monarchy legally into a popular monarchy, received a fatal blow through the Wilson notes.

And during the same hours in the night of October 30 a third portentous event took place. The stokers on the battleships at Kiel put out the fire under the boilers to prevent the fleet from advancing against the English enemy as ordered by the naval command. Here also the forces churned up by war and defeat clashed together. The decision of the naval command (Scheer), before the conclusion of the armistice, to relieve the Flanders front by an attack risking a sea battle with incalculable political consequences, had been taken without expressly informing or obtaining the consent of the government. It did not formally violate the newly reorganized imperial command authority, just promulgated on October 28, but was certainly a slap in the face of the new, and not only of the new but also of the old Bismarckian, system of government, which did not permit independent military decisions if they were of special political consequence. Military obstinacy, which had already transgressed its limits during the war, burst forth once again in heroic dimensions — for the possibility of an honorable death also stood before the eyes of the officers. It lacked, as is so often the case, a proper sense of proportion. The military ethic of the officers was quite different from that of the sailors. These latter were willing enough to ward off any attacks by the English, but the thought of voluntarily choosing an honorable death made them furious. Their morale exhausted, as it had been for a long time, they breathed a sigh of relief when the armistice request was made. They rightly suspected that the naval attack was not approved by Prince Max's government, and feared that the armistice was being torpedoed. They were not directly incited in their mutiny from the socialist side, but we have already seen that the appearance of the Independents in the country had influenced them, and that many socialists were among them. When, in a few days, they burst all the bonds of military discipline and hoisted red flags on the battleships, they most obviously were yearning for peace and not for the socialist vision of the future. Only a few of them knew what it meant. But at the very moment when the old military system burst from overexertion, the released forces instinctively seized upon the banner of that ideology which most bitterly opposed the old state. Many a cowardly deserter in the army likewise extenuated his deed with socialist slogans.

A colossal happening, absolutely unheard of in the history of the Prussian-German army, this mass mutiny could only succeed because the authority of the old powers among the starving population was already shaken by the admission of defeat and the further admission that they were themselves in need of fundamental reform. The real goal of this reform, to rally the people together for a last resistance against intolerable demands, was not achieved because the people were already too exhausted, and because the old rulers made mistakes which offset the effect of the reform. The delayed abdication of the Emperor and the unwise decision for a naval attack were the last errors of state committed by the old regime. By their untimely concurrence and effect, an out-and-out revolution became inevitable.

The Kiel movement, which began as a simple military mutiny, gradually acquired political content in the first days of November. The Majority Socialist Noske, who was sent to Kiel on November 4 to pacify and dam off the movement, felt himself powerless to restore the old discipline, but was at least strong enough to restore a certain order through being elected governor by the sailors themselves. But the mutiny was thereby given recognition as such, and the spreading news of its success had a powerful, seductive effect. The damming off did not succeed. Mere ripples of the movement, usually in the form of sailors dispatched along the highways in trucks, sufficed to uproot the old authorities in the great North German coastal cities, as well as in inland cities as far as Cologne, thus disrupting the vital bridge between the field army and the homeland. Everywhere workers' councils and soldiers' councils were quickly formed on the Russian model.

Without any direct connection to the Kiel movement, the revolution broke out in Munich on November 7. It was rooted in specifically Bavarian and Bavarian-peasant sentiments: the deep vexation among the country people about the long duration of the war, whose sacrifice of lives had hit Bavaria especially hard; the troublesome wartime government controls, which gave new life to anti-Prussian feeling; and lastly, the fear of direct invasion by the enemy after the collapse of the Italian front. The words, "Liebknecht is right," already resounded here in 1916 among people who were not in the least inclined toward socialism. Thus it is understandable that the Independent Socialist, Kurt Eisner, could be lifted to leadership at the large mass meeting of November 7 on the Theresian Fields, and, with the aid of a quickly formed workers', soldiers', and peasants' council, proclaim the "Democratic and Social Republic of Bavaria" on the night of November 8.

Only after the signal had been given in the North and South did Berlin also follow. Revolutionary agitation had existed here for a long time. The beginnings of secret revolutionary preparation go back, according to Ledebour's statement, to the year 1916. Richard Müller, the leader of the Berlin metal workers, directed his trade union into revolutionary channels. He and Emil Barth, a young radical hothead who was treated by his fellow party members as a vain fool, gathered together the "revolutionary shop stewards" [*revolutionäre Obleute*] in the Berlin factories. Altogether there were said to be in November 1918 several thousand organized people ready for a revolution in this city of millions. This would have meant little, had not the disposition of the masses become extremely unstable because of the armistice request and the question of the abdication. Upon the urging of the Social Democrats the October government made the mistake, by a grant of amnesty, of letting Liebknecht out of prison on October 21, thus permitting him to renew his wild agitation. At least the very dangerous connections of the revolutionary groups to the Russian embassy, which gave them funds and technical advice, were severed, upon Scheidemann's advice, by creating a pretext to expel the latter (November 6). Without knowledge of the Kiel movement, a decision had already been taken by a revolutionary committee on November 2 to open the attack in Berlin on November 4, but it was postponed until — at the latest — November 11 when it was learned that the workers in the smaller factories were not yet convinced. The arrest of one of the conspirators (Däumig) on November 8 produced the resolve to begin the venture immediately on November 9. Spartacus and the radical Independents were the driving forces.

The Majority Social Democrats were again placed in an infinitely difficult position. They saw the revolution coming and, according to their old principles, could not feel many regrets, but they certainly did not want a revolution now, because it could so easily get out of hand and lead to Bolshevism, which they abhorred. Their most capable leader, Ebert, said that he did not consider the time ripe for a republic and desired only the consolidation of the demo-

cratic monarchy. But the Party was prevented by the mentality of its followers from intervening against the revolution with the full weight of state power and the power of its own organization. Workers do not shoot at workers, it was often said — a phrase that explains much of what followed. Numerous elements from the Party had streamed over to the Independents in the course of the last year. The MSPD would have lost all its remaining popular influence, if it had not chosen flexible tactics to match the flexible mood of the masses. In order to bridle a wild nag, it has well been said, one must run along with it for a way. Thus, at first the policy of the MSPD focused on securing the abdication of the Emperor and Crown Prince. If this succeeded, it hoped to prevent the masses from further slipping away to the left.

The decisive day for everything that followed was November 6. In the Reich chancellory Groener sat opposite the leaders of the MSPD. Ebert demanded that the Emperor abdicate by the next day at the latest, and put one of his sons, Oscar or Eitel Friedrich, in his place. Groener rejected the abdication out of consideration for the front army and declared himself authorized to announce that neither of the princes would accept a regency if their father were forced to abdicate against his will. Ebert answered: "Then we come to a parting of the ways."

Seven years later (at the Munich stab-in-the-back trial) Groener regretted having spoken so. He should have said: "Herr Ebert, one man, one word"; perhaps it would still have been possible, he thought, to save the monarchy. He still acted as an officer on November 6 in the spirit of the historical monarchy whose existence now hung by a thread, not yet as a statesman, who occasionally breaks with tradition somewhat in order to preserve the essential continuity. But the call of destiny for purely statesmanlike action was to find a hearing with him a few days later.

A last attempt by the leaders of the MSPD to postpone the question of abdication until the conclusion of the armistice failed. They declared themselves unable to wait any longer because of the threat of revolution, and issued on November 7 an ultimatum that, as a condition for their staying in the government, the Emperor would have to abdicate before noon of November 8, and finally they extended the term until November 9 at 9 A.M.

The abdication did not come, Scheidemann left the government, and on November 9 the masses from the factories and trade unions, now encouraged also by the MSPD, rushed into the streets. The Naumburg Rifles, ordered to Berlin as an especially reliable unit, failed along with all other troops. The dam was broken. The government had neglected to train a completely dependable officers unit to protect it. In this helpless position, the Berlin Supreme Commander, General von Linsingen, saw that nothing else was left but to issue an order on November 9 (1:15 P.M.) not to shoot, so as to avert the useless shedding of blood. Only sporadic shooting ensued, mostly from the excited crowd.

Meanwhile even in Spa on the morning of November 9 the view that the abdication was inevitable was gaining support. Groener as well as Hindenburg declared that the already partly undermined army was no longer capable of a march against the revolutionary homeland. The Emperor decided at midday in favor of a politically and constitutionally impossible way out: to abdicate as Emperor, but to remain king of Prussia. A telephone message, however, had led Prince Max to believe that the abdication decision had already been made. That gave him the courage at noon to announce the abdication of the Emperor to the Berlin population. It was too late. In the afternoon around two o'clock, Scheidemann, overcome by the moment, proclaimed the German Republic from the Reichstag. At the same moment another leader of the MSPD was negotiating inside the Reichstag with the National Liberal under-secretary of state, Schiffer, about establishing a regency. And Ebert was deeply angered over Scheidemann's unauthorized action.

It would thus have been quite possible, as one can see, to save the monarchy by establishing a regency for the grandson of the Emperor. It could have survived, to be sure, only as a parliamentary figurehead monarchy, but the inner breach with the past would have been softened, and the reconciliation of the former ruling strata made easier — without of course forestalling all restorative spasms. One must always keep in mind that the politically decisive transformation of the state had already taken place, under the pressure of the military-political situation, before November 9. Actually, on November 9 only the republican cap and women's suffrage were added. Moreover, the collapse of the monarchy, which was followed by the collapse of all remaining German dynasties, opened up two significant political possibilities for the future: first to create a strong presidential force, on a democratic basis and independent of the accidents of dynastic birth, which could revitalize the good parts of Bismarck's constitutional monarchy; and second, to do away with the outmoded *Länder* and create the unitary state. Both would have been prevented by the continuance of the dynasties.

Three powerful blows following quickly one after the other — the armistice request, the third Wilson note, and the Kiel mutiny — brought about the sudden disappearance of authority, which directly brought on the ninth of November. This day was simultaneously the termination of a developmental process which ran through the entire war and the combined result of the most varied accidents, of fateful powers of compulsion and spontaneous responsible human action. Everything had at the same time a personal and a general character, an external and an internal side. Nothing came about only from the outside, or from the inside. The assertion that the revolution came "from the outside," namely that it was carried into the army by the agitation of the left-wing socialists, that from the homeland the army was stabbed in the back, is nothing more than a tendentious caricature of the course of events, with a certain grain of truth that is evident from our own story. The revolutionary agitation, which no one denies today, only became historically effective when the belief in victory had been shattered among the exhausted people and army, when the immunity of the body to the poison had disappeared. The socialist parties actually contributed to the causes of the revolution more through what they were than through what they did. Because of the very existence within the nation of extreme opposition parties that demanded political and social reorganization, they became the natural magnets for all dissatisfactions: war, hunger, annexationism, etc. That was inevitable and fateful. A stronger sense of destiny than the ruling classes possessed, would have been necessary to combat this fate effectively by human wisdom.

The ninth of November was, as we saw, only the end result of that great test of endurance, to which the old regime submitted itself in the World War. It entered the test with the imposing strength which universal military service, exploited to the utmost degree, gave it. This system, introduced exactly a century before, was a synthesis of military and popular — i.e., national as well as democratic — ideas. The developments of the nineteenth century up to the World War expanded the military element in it, preserved the national element, but weakened the democratic element. With this relative dosage, the system might have survived a mild conflict, but not a major one. When the endurance test of the war became more and more taxing, the rulers reached for the strongest means to exploit the military element still more completely (even subordinating policy to it), to raise the national element to a chauvinistic pitch, but to combat the democratic element — and that at a time when they had become even more dependent upon the masses because so much was asked of them. The system began to come apart and then broke

completely to pieces in the mutiny of the Kiel sailors. Not the old Bismarckian state but the hypertrophic military state of Ludendorff failed to pass the test. The war itself, however, proved to be the strongest of the revolutionary powers.

With the catastrophe of the old militarism, the strongest domestic pillar of the old political system had collapsed. But even a German military success could only have limited the democratization and not prevented it, after the crown promised the equal franchise for Prussia on July 11, 1917 (unless some powerful reaction had set in with incalculable consequences and recoils). The enormous tension of the social forces which the war had produced could only be quieted by the vent of democracy. The statesmanlike resolution to open this vent in time, before the addition of a humiliating external pressure, was unfortunately not to be found. Certainly a gigantic power would have been needed to carry it out against the obstinately rooted forces of conservative resistance.

The defeat completely paralyzed these conservative forces for the time being. The complete powerlessness with which they submitted to the Kiel mutiny and the ninth of November is one of the most surprising but essential features of the German Revolution. Only the commander of the battleship *König* gave his life in good Prussian fashion rather than submit to the mutineers. One of the most proven men of the war said later: "We were all used up. Our nerves were no longer up to such a new strain." But more profound causes for this behavior must also be considered. At that time the feeling was strong that one could no longer jam the spokes on the wheel of destiny, that the old was doomed to destruction and a completely new order was bound to come. And the new order could only have two forms, either democracy or Bolshevism. In this situation the Majority Social Democrats appeared as a bulwark against Bolshevism. One must now, said [Friedrich] Naumann classically at the time, fight the Bolsheviks with the Mensheviks. Everywhere a kind of silent mandate was given them, and all the old forces submitted.

This sudden yielding to the Revolution and the speedy subordination of all the organs of state to the new revolutionary officials must be explained not only as an instinctive resistance against Bolshevik chaos, by the concern to secure food supplies, by fear for private property, etc., but also by a profound transformation in the mentality of the upper strata during the preceding generations. There grew up a strange amalgamation of the old aristocratic monarchist feudal way of thinking and the bourgeois utilitarian. Many members of the upper middle class had become "feudalized" as reserve officers or in other ways, but had at the same time radiated their practical bourgeois mentality far into the old officialdom and the regular officer corps. Thus such apparently contradictory things could happen as the naval officers at first heroically contemplating an honorable death and then keeping their swords sheathed when surrounded by masses of mutineers. Therein they behaved in a manner similar to the mutineers themselves, who wanted nothing to do with heroic death.

This practical capitulation to the inevitable, which might be ennobled as the patriotic view that Germany's salvation lay in the consolidation of all non-Bolshevik forces, was now to determine all that followed.

Stab in the Back—A Nationalist View

GOTTFRIED ZARNOW

Gottfried Zarnow is the literary pseudonym of Ewald Moritz, a conservative-nationalist journalist who wrote a good deal of popular history in the interwar years. Like many German conservatives he welcomed the Nazi Revolution at first and continued to write until 1939 when he disappeared from view. The reader will notice, however, that his version of the *Dolchstoss* theory (written in 1933) does not contain the overt anti-Semitism that would permeate an outright Nazi account. Neither does he argue that Germany could have won the war but only that, without the traitorous thrust of the Social Democrats, it could have achieved an honorable compromise peace. Because Zarnow marshals legitimate historical evidence to support his view, it deserves serious—although critical—scrutiny. Why are the Social Democrats, rather than the Communists, the principal villains of the piece?

THE FIRST TEN days in November of 1918 will have stronger and more lasting consequences and will be more significant in German literature than the whole four years of the World War, with all the glow of the German victories whose equals are not to be found in history. In these ten days took place the most disgraceful treason known in the history of mankind. We will forget the misery of war, the hunger, the tears, but we will not — we must not — forget the cowardice, the treachery, and the guile of Germany's gravediggers.

A people which defends its honor can survive, but a people which revolts at the moment of the state's greatest need has ceased to be a people — to want to be a people.

If ever a people had to settle an account, then it was the one which the new national Germany settled in the spring of 1933 with its most dangerous enemy within — the Marxists [i.e., Social Democrats]. Every people possessing a resolute will for self-assertion will understand this settlement. It *provides the proof for the national neces-* *sity of the German Revolution of 1933.*

This book contains no history of the German collapse in November 1918. . . . The internal enemies of Germany, won over by the foe, used an opportune moment to stab us in the back: *to identify the perpetrators of this attack and to prove their guilt is the only task of the book.*

* * *

Was the German November Revolution really necessary? In other words, could it have made us any freer, when it swept over Germany like Greek fire, than we already were after the end of October 1918?

The perpetrators and exploiters of the Revolution, as disciples of Karl Marx, perpetually quoted his doctrine, but seem to have forgotten one of his opinions on revolution and its laws:

The time has long since passed for the superstition which ascribes revolution to the malice of a few agitators. Today everyone knows that wherever revolutionary uprisings appear a social need must be behind them whose satisfaction is prevented by outlived institutions.

From Gottfried Zarnow, *Der 9. November 1918* (Hamburg: Hanseatische Verlagsanstalt, 1933), pp. 7–8, 9–12, 74–78, 141–42, 144–51.

The German Revolution was the work of malicious agitators who kindled it, not to satisfy a "social need" or to remove "outlived institutions," but in order not to lose control over the masses and thereby their claim to power and its benefits.

These leaders, or rather foxes, demanded political rights for the people after the model of the western democracies. This demagogy can be exposed with the foxes' own words. In the official report of the [MSPD] party executive for the years 1914–1917 at the party congress in Würzburg, which the proletariat was hardly able to see, the following declaration is found: "The Entente may speak long and loud about the liberation of other nations — *in Germany there is not a single worker who does not see through the hypocritical game they play with democracy.*"

Was it in the interest of the fatherland and especially of the German worker for his leaders so to deafen him with demagogic phrases and make him dissatisfied?

But socialist revolutionary literature forces us to a third observation. In it is taught:

By revolution one understands the violent change of constitutional law by those citizens who do not hold state power.

The German revolution of Ebert, Scheidemann, etc., did not aim at the forceful alteration of the constitution, which had become as free as any in the world, but was directed against the defense of the country and was hardly carried out by citizens, for the German "revolutionaries" were tools of the [Second] International.

Until November 9, 1918 the German was a free man, determining his own destiny, but the Revolution has made him a pariah among the nations and a slave to the victors whose *only victory over us was the German Revolution itself.*

The mood of war weariness, cultivated by the Social Democrats since 1916 and finally elevated by them to an anti-war agitation, wore down the people's will to resist and created that army of "defeatists" who were punished in France but who became cabinet ministers in our country.

The Social Democratic state secretaries and under-secretaries of state, after their entrance into the German government on October 2, 1918, made not the slightest effort to remove the inner tensions of Germany, or at the least to do more than the previous German government had already done. It can also be proven from the government's white paper that Scheidemann, whose mouth had been open in the Reichstag and in many public meetings since the beginning of the war, made no suggestions at all for easing popular discontent even in direct response to questions put by Ludendorff in the great joint meeting of the cabinet and the Supreme Command on October 17, 1918.

Perhaps Scheidemann wanted to avoid suggestions for easing popular discontent in order not to cross up plans long discussed in the party executive of the SPD. The intransigent bearing of Scheidemann in this great and decisive meeting repeated itself on November 7 when he and Ebert delivered to Reich Chancellor Prince Max of Baden an unrealizable ultimatum with an impossible time limit. Prince Max of Baden writes about it in his memoirs:

When after the events in Kiel I saw the danger of civil war coming closer and closer, I sought an interview on Thursday with [Reichstag] Deputy Ebert and informed him that on the same evening I intended to travel to headquarters. He promised me to do his part to see that his party and the masses awaited the result of my visit. On the afternoon of the same day, however, *Herr Scheidemann and Herr Ebert delivered the Social Democratic ultimatum which forced me to turn in my resignation,* for it meant the collapse of my policy of using persuasion rather than force.

You will spare me the pain of speaking about the steps I undertook after my resignation request. *They had only one purpose, to permit the now unavoidable revolution to be carried out without a fratricidal struggle.*

I do not want to dispute with those who brought about and supported the overthrow, but I still believe today that the will of the people would have been carried through *without force* by means of a constituent assembly, for the calling of which we were honor-bound after the collapse of Austria. *I cannot rid myself of the idea that perhaps our workers and soldiers would have been patient twenty-four hours longer if the leaders from their midst had made clear to them the necessity of holding the home front, as it was clear to the soldiers that the battle front had to be held. Then the collapse would not have come one day before the armistice.*

The tragedy which Prince Max of Baden so carefully describes can be appreciated in its full horror only from the unanimous reports that on November 8 order still prevailed and work went on in all plants of Berlin, that Berlin seemed to hold fast despite the unrest burning everywhere else in Germany.

The Ebert-Scheidemann ultimatum ripped down the last dam, before which the revolutionary wave very probably would have come to rest. From a national point of view the ultimatum was a crime against the still fighting army, for Scheidemann coolly explained to the then Prussian interior minister Dr. Drews after his return from headquarters that *his party wanted to anticipate the Independents with the abdication demand, for the Independents wanted to pass over the question of the throne and proclaim a republic.*

Also Scheidemann's coup d'état at noon on November 9 (the proclamation of the Republic) was in no way the result of his own considered policy, much less the result of thorough consultation with statesmen and politicians; but when Scheidemann, over his "thin watery soup" in the dining hall of the Reichstag during the noon hour of November 9, heard that *Karl Liebknecht would proclaim a soviet republic [Räterepublik],* then he rushed in as before to nose out the competition. . . .

Against the superiority of the outside world the German army achieved fantastic things in this greatest of all wars in world history. By imperturbable devotion, ex-treme courage, and contempt for death, it surpassed all that history knows in its resistance against this excess of physical and material destructive power. And then came an indescribable plague brought on by a German treachery behind the front such as history has also never known. . . .

For 14 years a curse from a million throats rose to Heaven, a curse on all those who made Germany defenseless and without honor.

Democracy betrayed the nation and was marked by history with the death sign.

* * *

The war aims policy of the Social Democratic leaders was from the beginning not a matter of principle but only of tactics: it was subject to change. The German working masses on the other hand were unconditionally national in feeling and desire. Discord was artificially produced and spread by the ambition of their party bosses. This political and spiritual discord became a source of strength to our enemies. Here lay that inner breach which became more important to the course of the war than the military front.

Most Social Democratic leaders could not give unreserved support to complete victory for Germany. They did not want it because an undisputed victory, in their opinion, would have brought the complete dominion of "Junkerdom" and "capitalism" and destroyed for a long time their hopes of taking power in Germany. Thus can one explain the position of the Party leaders after December 1914, their support not of a victorious peace but of a peace of reconciliation.

This call for ending the scarcely started war was an outrage against our people, a crime whose actual consequences must have been clear from the beginning to those responsible. Thus began *the treason from within the ranks of our own people.* For this heavy accusation Social Democracy delivers its own conclusive proof: official party literature, "printed as a manuscript," and therefore not meant for the public.

In September 1916 a Reich conference of the German Social Democratic Party took place in Berlin. There the Reichstag deputies Ebert and Scheidemann reported on "the policies of the party" and the "activity of the party executive." The speeches published by the party executive were carefully corrected before printing because of the censorship (the preface indicates this); what was released for publication was therefore the least that was said.

The relevant portion of Ebert's speech reads:

After the outbreak of the war the party leadership began afresh and continued unceasingly in its endeavors to bring about contact and understanding with the International. In September 1914 members of the party executive in Switzerland tried to get in touch with the French party. The attempt did not succeed — not through our fault. Several weeks later the Dutch party declared itself ready to take over the functions of the international office and to introduce conciliatory action among the parties of the belligerent nations. The suggestion was first submitted to us after it had found the support of the three Scandinavian parties. We welcomed this suggestion, as did our Austrian friends. *The French party on the other hand raised a violent protest against it.* . . .

Thus it was perfectly clear that both the French and English socialists approved continuation of the war against Germany. That should have reassured us in accepting the same policy: to pursue *war, victory,* and only then *peace,* in order to show abroad the inner unity of the German people. For this priority leading Social Democrats themselves set up principles that the government could not have formulated more sharply, and if they were not kept but rather consciously violated, then this is the confirmation of the systematic gravedigging performed by our Social Democrats. . . .

Scheidemann wrote [in 1916]:

Our opponents place their hope for victory in the unity and war spirit of their countries and in the discord and lack of war spirit in our country. These hopes must be destroyed, the sooner the better.

Whoever commits acts that strengthen the hope of our opponents, helps to prolong the war.

Thus . . . Scheidemann unambiguously and unreservedly took the view that whoever transgresses these boundaries commits high treason, or at least treason against the people.

The peace question split Germany from first to last into two camps. Scheidemann certainly knew this and his tacking about from one standpoint to the other can only be explained through the needs of his party. For him as for his opponents *there was only one goal, namely to see the party and himself in the saddle of power at the end of the war.* Till then he had to seesaw back and forth: on one side he had to ingratiate himself with bourgeois circles through patriotic speeches, and he had to be able to prove to the comrades on the other side his international and pacifist convictions.

Scheidemann could do even more: he was able to satisfy those radical elements that wanted peace at any price, followed by revolution. At the party congress in Würzburg (October 1917) he threw these people a little morsel.

That which we want and for which we struggle is the unheard of, the great, the new. It is the elevation of all mankind to a higher cultural level, to an international society of peoples, and to socialism. Thus this world war appears to us only as the mighty prelude to a still mightier event, a spiritual and social revolution such as the world never has experienced.

He concluded with the vow: "We will march and — if must be — we will storm. Forward!"

The enemy used such peace and revolution mongering by the Social Democratic leaders for their propaganda leaflets and dropped them over the German trenches and hinterland. . . .

Concern about the party membership,

not concern about the future of the nation, occupied the party leaders from the beginning of the war, actually in two directions: what consequences does our attitude toward the war have for the party and trade unions, and what can we expect from the war for the party and the International? The then editor of *Vorwärts,* Heinrich Ströbel, answered the latter question on February 23, 1915 and provided with it the key for the judgment of Social Democratic tactics: *"I declare quite openly that a complete victory for the Reich would not be in the interest of Social Democracy."*

Right! The entire war aims policy of Social Democracy can be summarized in this single sentence and all speeches for and against the war (or peace) can fall under the same formula.

* * *

Could Germany have won a bearable, at least honorable peace?

What did the German Revolution destroy of the people and the state?

These questions embrace the greatest recorded tragedy of a people; earlier peoples may have gone to ruin, but not such a great people and not through their own fault.

The perpetrators of the German Revolution named in this book try to evade responsibility with the explanation that the military collapse brought on the political revolution as a consequence. They go even further, namely with the assertion that only the acceptance of the armistice conditions preserved the German army from destruction. To demonstrate this, much ink has been wasted and many proofs offered. This fact alone proves the bad conscience of the guilty, who want to ease their burden and cleanse themselves before history. Whether or not Germany was betrayed by Germans hinges upon the presentation of a convincing answer [to the question of military collapse].

That Germany could no longer win a victory after America's entry into the war was as certain to all Germans, including those militarily responsible, as two times

two is four. (This primitive equation is intentionally chosen.) Only the question remains whether the German front could have kept up resistance until the achievement of honorable armistice conditions.

Reich Chancellor Prince Max of Baden expressed himself in such a way that we are justified in calling the German revolutionaries traitors.

After the war the German military leaders Hindenburg and Ludendorff spoke positively before the Reichstag committee of inquiry about the possibilities of military resistance: "Despite the heavy demand on troops and leaders, despite the numerical superiority of the enemy, we could have led the struggle to a happy end if there had been a solid and unified collaboration of army and home front."

"Army and homeland!" The army held out, but the home front?

Exactly seven years later Ludendorff's successor, General Groener, after the fullest examination and with uncontested authority as an expert, testified in court on the same question. . . .

We could still muster resistance, that question must be settled. What was the advantage if the army held together? It was that we would not have been obliged to accept the peace terms if we stood behind the Rhine with a tolerably strong army, and *it is therefore correctly said that the outbreak of the revolution deprived the army of the possibility of fighting at least for better peace terms behind the strong river barrier. Always on the supposition that the home front remained obedient and brave.*

This resistance behind the Rhine could have had enormous consequences. It could have secured our Eastern frontier. Naturally we could not defend the Rhineland — that had to be sacrificed first to the enemy — but perhaps we could have succeeded thereby in bringing back Eastern troops for support, gradually pulling back the troops in the Ukraine to defend the Eastern frontier, and shaping things more favorably at the Brenner and elsewhere.

Because of the decisive significance of this testimony, for General Groener is politically a democrat, it had to be reproduced in detail; and it coincides with the opinion of the French Generalissimo Foch which will be given later.

From this testimony alone one can perceive the enormous tragedy that descended upon Germany by the will of its most undutiful sons. We ourselves, however, are not yet satisfied with the evidence so far presented, and we shall dispense with any more from the German side, for the enemy has testified in favor of the German army more than is necessary to convict the traitors.

* * *

The London weekly, *The New Statesman,* wrote on October 26, 1918 about the strong signs of fatigue on the enemy side:

The season for combat is almost over. All the armies of the Allies are seemingly worn out. British troops are the only ones in recent weeks to show themselves capable of moving ahead in those sectors where the Germans offer stubborn resistance. Each week increases the prospect that Hindenburg will be able to pull back his forces without serious loss to rear positions where they can stand through the winter without great risk. The eventual line, if not for the winter, then for the spring would be the line of the Maas. Its natural strength is very great and would be enormously increased by three months of winter work. The Maas line means a very significant shortening of the front and would thus permit the German reserve divisions to increase again to a considerable number, at least for purposes of defense.

So generous is the recognition given voluntarily by the enemy to our German front soldiers, if not to their highest leaders. Who does not lower his eyes before the unnamed heroes of the World War?

It was perhaps only a few days or weeks that separated Germany from a compromise peace.

The foreign press opinion cited here has been strengthened factually in later years by the utterances of enemy army leaders and politicians, so that we, the mourners, today have the choice of accusing, either the blindness of the military command, the pitiable weakness of the government, or the traitorous role of the German revolutionaries.

The following reports of the foreign military and politicians may rightly be viewed as the heaviest burden their opponents on our side must bear.

The Commander-in-Chief of the English troops fighting in France, General Sir Douglas Haig, writes in his final report on December 21, 1918:

It must be understood that our advance against the active resistance of even a beaten and demoralized foe would have been quite protracted. The difficulties of supply, under which we would have been forced to move large quantities of ammunition forward, would have grown worse in several ways. Bridges, roads, and railways in front of us would have been destroyed or prepared for destruction by time bombs. Huge losses would . . . have resulted.

The former British Munitions Minister, Winston Churchill, depicts the position of the German army at the end of October 1918 in terms similar to the English Commander-in-Chief:

For the Germans now had, apart from all strategic and tactical measures, a simple mechanical means to slow down pursuit, whose full exploitation would certainly have provided them breathing space till spring 1919. They had invented . . . time fuses; . . . the Allied armies would have been able to advance against the German frontier only after they had rebuilt the entire railway system lying in between. This could surely not have happened before the end of the year. A six-month breathing space would have been gained by the Germans before the full power of the Allied armies developed at their frontier and could threaten them with a hostile invasion. This time would have sufficed to choose strong positions, to fortify them, and to employ all the remaining might of the nation for the defense of this area. . . .

How differently the armistice conditions would have read if the German army had known no revolution and no traitors at their

*backs and the feared German navy had re-
mained ready and willing to fight. . . .*

The perpetrators of the German Revolution might dispute about their guilt or lack
of guilt before the French Marshal Foch
set forth his views. This he did in August
1928 to a correspondent of the Vienna
Neue Freie Presse. The opinion advanced
by Marshal Foch is high praise for the
German army, an annihilating criticism of
its leaders, and, what is not expressed by
him, an affirmation of the question: Was
the German Revolution the greatest crime
against a people known to the history of
all nations?

That is sufficient reason to quote ver-
batim the decisive portion of the *Neue
Freie Presse* report. Foch explained among
other things:

I mentioned already that even in the spring
of 1918 Germany could have won the war. If
the Germans had pressed forward to Amiens
they would have cut off the English from the
French army. But even after the offensive of
General Mangins on July 18, 1918 Germany's
situation was not desperate. I confess I cannot
understand from a strategic standpoint why
General Ludendorff did not withdraw to a
Metz-Meuse-Brussels-Antwerp line around
August 20, 1918. My preparations were aimed
at an attack on the "Hindenburg Line" and
if the German army had withdrawn to the
shorter, straighter line just mentioned, I would
have been forced to begin everything all over
again. This strategic retreat could have prolonged the war for a year, and in critical times
many unexpected things can happen in the
course of a year. I can nevertheless understand
that General Ludendorff did not want to take
it upon himself to order this strategic retreat,
which would have been an admission of evident inferiority and would have required leaving behind important, irreplaceable war material. I would go even further and assert that
in November 1918 Germany could have held
its ground behind the Rhine. If the German
people had had a Gambetta, the war would
have been prolonged . . . and who knows . . . ?

At this point the correspondent of the
Viennese paper interrupted Marshal Foch
and reminded him that the example of

Gambetta proves that heroic resistance by a
militarily beaten people only serves to prolong war needlessly. France lost at Sedan
on September 2, 1870. Everything that
happened thereafter was only a prolonga-
tion of the death agony.

"All that is true," responded Marshal
Foch, "nevertheless I believe that a people
which does not want to be beaten, need not
be beaten. In November 1918, needless to
say, Germany had no prospect for victory
any more, *but if its army had made a stand
behind the Rhine many things would have
turned out differently."* . . .

Here at this point justice must be done
to a statesman who saw the tragedy coming
in those heavy autumn days, but who was
no longer able to avert it. When the Supreme Command urged the Reich government on October 1 to send out an armistice
offer immediately, Chancellor Prince Max
of Baden asked on October 3 the self-evi-
dent counter-question: "How long can the
army hold the enemy on the other side of
the German frontier?" The Supreme Command did not answer this question but
merely made its urgent demand still more
urgent, a proof that it was completely im-
prisoned by the feeling of hopelessness and
futility.

On January 28, 1926 in the Reichstag
committee of inquiry, the so-called "Dittmann Committee" that investigated the
sailors' mutinies of 1917 and 1918, diary
entries and military-political observations
were read from the book (then in press) of
Prince Max of Baden. After recognizing
the strategic and psychological utility of the
naval attack planned in the North Sea for
October 28 (1918) the Prince continues:

But I admit that when once the decisive
battle had been determined on, it was the duty
of the Naval Command to work itself up to
the temper of unshakable confidence in victory. And even had I not been carried away by
these soaring hopes, the following considerations would still have led me to give my assent
in principle to the naval operation:
If we should win — and this, considering
our leadership, the training of the crews, and

the superiority of our materiel, was not inconceivable — the hard-pressed army and the civil population whose impatience under its sufferings was daily growing, would receive a powerful impulse to hold out. After a German naval victory the revolution and capitulation of November 9 and 11 would have been almost a psychological impossibility; on the other hand it must be said that such a defeat would have bound the English more closely than ever to our mortal enemy France.

But should our navy suffer a glorious defeat, yes, and even if this last cruise were really to be a "Death Cruise," even then its desirability from a military-political point of view must certainly be conceded. This sacrifice would have been a moral force, capable of putting to shame the many disaffected and despairing folk who would not have been able to escape its influence. I have been justly reminded of Thermopylae. . . .

No Kiel, no revolution; no revolution, no capitulation on November 11!

To this heavy accusation the reply is always made that the "National Defense" scheme was in any case senseless and purposeless.

To this I am bound to say that one must take account not only of the material resources, but also of the will of the enemy peoples. Had it for instance been a case of conquering Alsace-Lorraine, then the Allied rulers would have been in a position to impose on their peoples years more of war, now that the final victory was no longer in doubt.

But on November 11 quite another situation was conceivable. Suppose the Wilson conditions accepted; suppose the evacuation of Belgium and Northern France, yes, and even of Alsace-Lorraine conceded — *and suppose the demand for our disarmament answered by the "No!" of a nation resolute to fight to the uttermost.*

In this case it is my firm conviction that our will to fight a struggle of desperation needed only to last a few weeks to make the enemy rue his demand for our annihilation.

From their peoples an overpowering cry would have gone up to heaven: "Are we to

sacrifice hundreds of thousands more before we are over the Rhine — simply to extort Foch's armistice conditions? The price is too high!" From the home front this feeling would have leaped the gap and spread among the Allied armies, which would have had to contend with the worst season of the year and with terrific difficulties of transport. And in the end the will to take the offensive would have been extinguished.

Fresh negotiations would then presumably have been initiated. The armistice terms which we should then have had to accept would have been very hard; but my belief is they would not have handed Germany bound hand and foot to the Versailles Diktat.

And yet there were circles which boasted of their gains. Hermann Müller declared: *"On the day of the armistice Social Democracy reaped the fruits of the World War."*

The question whether the armistice offer was militarily necessary must be answered by soldiers; outside their competence lies the more important decision: how to return it in a diplomatically clever way to the senders and how to present it to the public. The persons who acted here arbitrarily and therefore failed have drawn a guilt upon themselves that would be unbearable for patriots.

Did we put down our arms too early trusting in Wilson's Fourteen Points or hoping to escape military defeat?

Idle questions, for the enemy could calculate with a slide rule when the revolution would descend upon us and knock our weapons from our hands.

The armistice commission left Berlin on November 6, 1918, crossed the enemy line on November 7 after 7 P.M., was obliged to board a train on the evening of the eighth, and woke up on the morning of the ninth in the forest of Compiègne —

In Germany during those same days the revolutionary sparks leapt from city to city, igniting the fuel that had been systematically piled up for years.

Foch could wait until the news of revolution at home had speeded up the retreat of the army, until there was no more holding, until no dishonorable conditions — no power in the world — could check the panic.

TIME WON — WAR WON!

The peace was dictated by an enemy that trembled before our German soldiers for four years, and because he could not hope to win against them in open battle — in many places at the front since summer 1918 the ratio had become ten to one — carried on the most ruthless war known to the history of mankind: *a war against old men, women, and children.*

The peace was dictated by an enemy who as victor was ruled only by contemptible feelings: the inhuman drive for revenge, distorted by a lingering fear of an opponent who had defied the world and who, lying on the ground, still inspired fear, for thus read Point Sixteen of the armistice conditions: "Blockade remains in effect. German ships may continue to be seized." The thirst for revenge smoldered and stifled everything, even the humanity and the respect which the victor since the gray dawn of history has not denied the vanquished.

In the first ten days of November 1918 Germany sank into a defenselessness and incapacity that even Jena did not reach in the year of degradation 1806.

The answer to the first question: "Could Germany win for itself a bearable, at least honorable peace?" is to be answered with a yes which no one can convincingly refute.

The answer to the second question: "What did the German Revolution destroy of the people and the state?" the enemy answers daily, yearly, since November 10, 1918 with undisguised abuse of the military superiority that fell into his lap on November 9, 1918.

Therewith began the second act of the German tragedy.

Unsuccessful Proletarian Revolution— A Communist View

ROLAND BAUER

Roland Bauer, at one time Director of the Institute of Marxism-Leninism in Berlin, is a prominent East German Communist historian who has written on the development of the Second International. The present essay, composed in 1958 for a 40th anniversary discussion of the November Revolution, reflects the latest revision of Communist historiography. As Bauer explains, during the anti-German years of the Stalin period (inaugurated by Stalin himself in his famous *History of the Communist Party of the Soviet Union: Short Course*), the German November Revolution was denied the status of a genuine working-class uprising. In this post-Stalin rehabilitation, Bauer discusses the Marxist criteria for appraising revolutions and returns to the original Communist judgment that 1918 constituted an abortive proletarian revolution.

THE NOVEMBER REVOLUTION was one of the mightiest mass movements in the history of the German people, and one of the greatest struggles of the German proletariat. But it did not lead to victory. As Ernst Thälmann very rightly said, the tragedy of the Revolution of 1918 lay "in the discrepancy between the matured objective revolutionary conditions on the one hand and the subjective weakness of the German proletariat, due to the lack of a clear-sighted Bolshevist party, on the other."

This contradiction between the objective and subjective conditions of the November Revolution produced manifestations scarcely to be encountered in other revolutions. The Revolution broke out against the will of the right-wing SPD and USPD leaders, yet they were the ones to win primary influence in the workers' and soldiers' councils as well as in the governments brought forth by the upheaval. The masses of the German working class wanted to establish a socialist order of society but were not clear as to how to go about it. They believed the demagogic and deceitful ma-

neuvers of the government of People's Commissars, who spoke of socialism and socialization but in fact pursued a counter-revolutionary policy. The majority of the workers' and soldiers' councils — i.e., the real bearers of the new state power — supported the calling of a National Assembly, thus giving up the positions of power they had just won, while at the same time the most progressive sections of the working class struggled outside the councils against the National Assembly and for extending and securing the power of the councils.

Appraising the character of the Revolution of 1918 is secondly complicated by the fact that Germany, though in capitalist terms one of the most developed countries in the world, still retained several feudal vestiges as a consequence of its incomplete bourgeois revolution in 1848. The tasks of the socialist revolution were fused together with the elimination of these feudal and half-feudal remnants. Thus the working class came forth both with purely socialist demands like socialization of the means of production and with such demands as the

From Roland Bauer, "Über den Charakter der Deutschen November Revolution," *Zeitschrift für Geschichtswissenschaft*, VI (1958), 136–42, 150–57, 167–68.

elimination of the monarchy, of the state of siege, of restrictions on the right to organize, etc. These latter demands, usually raised in bourgeois revolutions, were essentially fulfilled by the November Revolution (except for the agrarian question), but the socialist revolution bogged down at the very beginning and was then bloodily suppressed by the counter-revolution of early 1919.

The appraisal of the November Revolution is thirdly complicated because it actually fragmented itself into many partial actions separated from one another in time and place. In contrast to France in 1789 and 1848 and to Russia in 1905 and 1917, where the revolutions began in the capital city and then spread out over the whole country, the November Revolution began at the periphery of Germany, engulfed one area after another, and only at the end reached Berlin. Because of this peculiar course of events, the old state and power apparatus located in Berlin was at first able to organize measures against the Revolution without much disturbance, and when the mass movement could no longer be halted it was still able to turn over the government to Ebert at the last minute.

But even when the revolutionary movement had embraced all of Germany, it still had no central authority to link up and lead the struggles of the masses. Therefore the degree of upheaval in the first days of the Revolution differed greatly in the various cities and *Länder,* depending on particular power relations and local conditions. . . .

Bourgeois and even Social Democratic historians are completely helpless in appraising the character of the November Revolution, because they proceed from individual events and examples rather than from the objective situation and the analysis of class relationships in German society. Either they avoid generalizations and socio-economic appraisals or else they develop them into unsolvable contradictions.

Marxist historians, in analyzing the Revolution, proceed not merely from individual examples and facts but from the totality of social and political conditions in Germany before and during the Revolution, from the objective requirements of the Revolution, the socio-economic basis of the Revolution, the fundamental content of the class struggle, etc. On this ground the Marxists of the twenties and thirties were absolutely right in asserting that the popular struggle of the German masses in 1918–1919, with the working class at the lead, bore a socialist, proletarian character. They presented the view that the November Revolution was, according to its character, a socialist and proletarian revolution which suffered defeat or — to put it more exactly — did not achieve victory, not even temporarily, because it bogged down along the way as a consequence of the betrayal of the right-wing SPD and USPD leaders and the immaturity of the German working class. These Marxists did not regard the November Revolution as isolated from revolutionary movements in other countries, but saw in it a very essential part of the first stage of the proletarian world revolution introduced by the beginning of the general crisis of capitalism and the Great Socialist October Revolution. . . .

With the appearance of the *History of the Communist Party of the Soviet Union: Short Course,* the majority of Marxist historians gradually adopted a different interpretation. Since the November Revolution, through its great weaknesses, did not lead to the victory of the proletariat, but only eliminated the monarchy and several feudal vestiges still remaining in 1918, it was from then on judged by its results to be a bourgeois revolution. Corresponding to this changed evaluation of the character of the Revolution, many other subsidiary questions — such as the role of the councils — were differently appraised. This led to a series of unjustified exaggerations because, in evaluating the Revolution as bourgeois, many complicated problems were frequently oversimplified or viewed schematically. The councils were judged by many historians to be nothing more than organs of counter-revolution. A number of Marxists even questioned whether a proletarian revolution was possible in Germany in 1918. They spoke only of the democratic tasks of the Revolution. Others criticised the Spartacus League for errors they did not even make, and finally there were even Marxist historians who doubted the democratic character of the Revolution and disputed whether the November Revolution of 1918 was really a popular uprising. . . .

In present-day discussion essentially two tendencies have crystalized. One still takes the standpoint that the November Revolution had the character of a bourgeois-democratic revolution. The other, embracing a larger and larger group, holds the old opinion of the Marxist historians that the Revolution had the character of an unsuccessful proletarian revolution.

The complexity of the November Revolution, the history of Marxist historiography on the character of the Revolution, and the experience of present-day discussion all show that a profitable resumption of the discussion can only be achieved if the participants agree what Marxism understands by the concept "character of a revolution" and what factors and impulses determine this character. . . .

*   *   *

According to the conceptions of Marx, Engels, and Lenin, what determines the character of a revolution, whether it is bourgeois or proletarian, is not the result of the revolution but in the first instance the totality of its social, economic, and political requirements and its objective class content, the class character of the power struggle in the revolution.

In contrast to bourgeois and Social Democratic historians, most Marxists take the stand that all the objective preconditions for a socialist revolution were at hand in Germany in 1918. But since the German bourgeois revolution of 1848 was not completed and several feudal remnants still existed in 1918, some Marxist historians are of the opinion that it was not imme-

diately possible at that time to undertake socialist tasks. They assert that the November Revolution first had to go through a bourgeois-democratic stage and only after accomplishing these tasks could it be led to the socialist stage. Thus, for example, W. F. Schälike writes: The tasks of the November Revolution consisted in "overthrowing the monarchy, . . . solving the agrarian question, and winning bourgeois-democratic freedoms." Drawing the logical conclusion, she believes that it was not possible in 1918 to go beyond the bourgeois-democratic stage, because the tasks of the Revolution in the first instance had a bourgeois-democratic rather than a socialist character. Such an interpretation stands in flat contradiction to the historical facts. In a purely factual sense, Schälike misunderstands both the objective social-economic requirements of the November Revolution and the fundamental character of the epoch in which it took place. In a political sense, her view effectively acknowledges the correctness of the right-wing SPD and USPD leaders in 1918. For if the Revolution had primarily to accomplish bourgeois-democratic tasks, then the policy of the right-wing SPD, USPD, and trade-union leaders corresponded to objective historical necessity. It follows that their policy was essentially right and the reproaches still made against them today are not justified. The policy of the Spartacus League, which oriented the proletariat immediately to the struggle for socialism, must logically have been false, while the accusation of putschism raised by the enemies of the working class against this policy must have been justified.

In fact, Germany in 1918 stood on the eve of a proletarian revolution. It was one of the most developed imperialist countries of Europe and, with respect to its state-monopolistic character, it was even the most developed country in the whole world. The material forces of production in German society stood in sharpest contradiction to the existing capitalist relations of production. At the same time the high degree of social production and the state-monopolistic stage of German imperialism had created all the objective material preconditions for the dissolution of capitalism. Lenin pointed precisely to the example of Germany when, in his famous work, *The Threatening Catastrophe and How to Fight It,* he wrote that "state-monopoly capitalism is the fullest *material* preparation for socialism, is its threshold, is that rung on the historical ladder between which rung and the one called socialism *there are no intermediate rungs.*"

Both social and political conditions in 1918 were ripe for a socialist revolution. By far the numerically strongest class in German society was the proletariat. The fundamental class contradiction of German society for a period of 50 years prior to the November Revolution was the contradiction between capital and labor. Not only the workers, however, but also the masses of working peasants and urban middle classes found themselves in flat opposition to the ruling class of monopolists and Junkers; for they too were oppressed, just like the working class, both economically and politically by the possessors of power. Certainly Germany was still a monarchy in 1918. But that changes nothing, for this monarchy was no feudal state, but rather the typical state of Junker-bourgeois imperialism. The nobility had the principal influence in the state apparatus. But it was no longer economically a feudal nobility, defending itself against the assault of the bourgeoisie, but rather a Junker-bourgeois nobility peculiar to Germany. These nobles — in other words, Junkers — were capitalist rather than feudal landowners, and moreover participated in many imperialistic industrial and financial undertakings. On the other side, typical monopoly capitalists were ennobled. Apart from the usual differences that always appear within the ruling class, called forth in capitalism by different profit interests, there were no longer any essential antagonisms after the beginning of imperialism between the bourgeois Junkers and the imperialistic great bourgeoisie. Junkerdom and monopoly capital were united on the principal questions of domestic and foreign policy. At the same time, one must not forget that the basic tasks of the bourgeois revolution had been achieved in Germany since 1871, even if this was done in a reactionary way by Bismarck. Consequently, as Lenin said, "the question of a general *democratic* revolution in Germany died." In the following decades Germany became "a fully capitalist, relatively free state with a stable constitution and universal suffrage." And with the development of imperialism, proletarian revolution became the order of the day, and its outbreak was speeded up, not retarded, by the World War of 1914–1918.

In this connection it must finally be mentioned that the November Revolution broke out one year after the Great Socialist October Revolution — i.e., in the period of the general crisis of the capitalist system, in the epoch of the proletarian world revolution — and this decisively determined the course of the 1918 Revolution in Germany. The victory of the Russian workers and peasants in October 1917 mobilized the German working class against its own exploiters, influenced the social direction and goals of this struggle, and provided in the form of the councils the models of revolutionary organization.

From all this it follows that Germany in 1918 was ripe for the immediate struggle for socialism. The principal task of the Revolution was to destroy the bases of German imperialism and militarism, to smash the Junker-bourgeois state apparatus, and to establish the power of the workers and peasants; i.e., the dictatorship of the proletariat. At the same time, the Revolution had to eliminate the remaining feudal vestiges and accomplish the unresolved task of the bourgeois revolution (agrarian reform) as subsidiary parts of the socialist revolution. For all practical purposes, the same situation existed here as in the Russian October Revolution, which in the first months after the victory of the workers and peasants had to bring the unresolved tasks of the bourgeois revolution to completion.

Thus it is clearly proven that the November Revolution, according to its socio-economic setting, was not a bourgeois revolution. It did not need to go through a bourgeois-democratic stage, as some historians assert, but was an unambiguous proletarian and socialist revolution. . . .

"A bourgeois revolution," says Lenin, "is a revolution that does not proceed beyond the framework of the bourgeois — i.e., capitalist — social and economic order. A bourgeois revolution expresses capitalism's need to develop and does not destroy the basis for that development, but on the contrary broadens and deepens it." For this reason . . . he said that the Revolution of 1905 was bourgeois because what it sought and what its forces could achieve did not go beyond the changes realized in the French bourgeois revolution of 1792–1793.

We do not, however, encounter either of these characteristics in the November Revolution. It did not express capitalism's need to develop, but rather the historical necessity to establish and develop a new, a socialist, society. For a variety of reasons, however, the working class was too weak to help the laws of history break through. Judged by its objective class content, the Revolution of 1918 — in spite of its great weaknesses — was a revolution not in the interest of the bourgeoisie but in the interest of the proletariat against the domination of the monopolists and Junkers, a revolution of the working class. It did not serve to broaden the basis of capitalism; precisely the opposite, it moved in the direction of destroying capitalism. Since it did not lead to victory, our publications on the November Revolution usually give these indisputable facts little notice, or even forget them completely. . . .

Such interpretations overemphasize certain sides of the Revolution while leaving other no less important phenomena out of consideration. It is true that the working class, as a consequence of its splitting up into three tendencies, of the opportunistic policy of the right-wing SPD, USPD, and trade-union leaders, and of the absence of

a Marxist-Leninist party, was insufficiently prepared for the approaching revolution. Both before and during the November Revolution, the majority of the working class did not have a clear conception of the fundamental tasks of a proletarian revolution. This inadequate maturity on the part of the subjective factor was the greatest weakness and likewise the principal reason for the defeat of the November Revolution. But one must not so exaggerate this weakness . . . as to negate all the conscious preparatory work of the left-wing element on the eve of the Revolution. One must not go so far in stressing weaknesses . . . as to ignore the fact that the November Revolution — even if unsuccessful — was directed not merely against the monarchy but against the entire capitalist system.

Even before the October Revolution, the Spartacus group and the Bremen left radicals had set their course toward proletarian revolution, in accordance with the resolutions of the Basel Congress of the Second International. After the Russian February Revolution, the idea of councils also came to life in the German working class. The October Revolution not only gave new impulse to this movement but raised it qualitatively to a higher plane. The demands put forth in the January strike of 1918 (overthrow the government, smash the power of the bourgeoisie, people's revolution, etc.) show clearly that the vanguard of the German working class was orienting the masses toward socialist revolution. The Spartacus group and the left radicals comprehended the significance of the councils as fighting organs of the proletarian revolution. Especially after the summer of 1918, in innumerable handbills, they called the German working class to the struggle for power in the state and in the economy, and to the organization of workers' and soldiers' councils. . . .

Thus prepared by the October Revolution and by the active work of the revolutionary wing of the German workers' movement, the November Revolution was characterized from the very first day, wherever it took root, by the formation of workers' and soldiers' councils. In order to prevent this, the ruling class decided in early November to organize armed citizens' defense units against the "threatening danger of Bolshevism." But neither the Revolution nor the formation of workers' and soldiers' councils could be halted. On November 8 the Revolution engulfed the centers of industry. Workers' and soldiers' councils were formed in Bielefeld, Krefeld, Essen, Düsseldorf, Kassel, Cologne, Mannheim, Augsburg, Nuremberg, Magdeburg, Halle, Leipzig, Dresden, Chemnitz (now Karl-Marx-Stadt), and other cities. Berlin followed on November 9 along with the larger cities of Silesia, and Pomerania, East, and West Prussia on November 10. With that the movement had encompassed all Germany. The immediately visible results of the upheaval were the banishment of the Emperor, the kings, and the princes, the dissolution of existing governments, and the formation of workers' and soldiers' councils. Many Marxist historians therefore compare the November Revolution with the 1917 February Revolution in Russia. Although there are many similarities of form, such a comparison is not correct because of the basically different class forces underlying each of the two revolutions. In its first period, the November Revolution was directed against the monarchy as the ruling instrument of the bourgeoisie and the capitalistic Junkers, and was composed of two class forces — the working class and a portion of the petty bourgeoisie. Its principal demands were peace, democracy, and socialism. The Russian February Revolution was directed against tsarism as the ruling instrument of the *feudal* landowners, and began as a coalition of three classes — the proletariat, the peasantry, and the liberal bourgeoisie along with Entente capital. Its principal demands were peace, freedom, bread, and land. In Germany the bourgeoisie was already in power before the Revolution, while in Russia it was the victory of the Revolution that placed state power in the hands of the bourgeoisie.

Neither during the Revolution nor in the next few months did the Bolsheviks lead an immediate campaign for the introduction of socialism, while the Spartacus League struggled for the political power of the working class, for the victory of the socialist revolution.

* * *

If we review the entire course of the Revolution, the following conclusion presents itself: although the November Revolution did not transcend the level of a bourgeois-democratic revolution in its objective result (except for the council republics in Bremen and Bavaria), it is fully justified to define it, according to its basic class content, according to its character, as a proletarian revolution. It was the first attempt of the German proletariat to seize state power and to establish the political dominion of the working class. If the revolutionary representatives of the German working class were not successful in 1918–1919 in securing the positions won in the first assault and in developing the councils into organs of proletarian state power, organs of the dictatorship of the proletariat, then this must be ascribed to the following factors: the clever tactics of the well-organized German bourgeoisie, which had learned much from the Russian experiences; the participation of the entire international counter-revolution in the struggle against the power of the councils; and the inexperience and lack of clarity, the insufficiently developed class consciousness of the majority of the German proletariat. Since this majority remained under the influence of the right-wing SPD, USPD, and trade-union leaders, it recognized neither the fundamental tasks of the socialist revolution nor the theoretical significance of the councils as organs of proletarian state power. At the same time, great masses of hitherto nonpolitical people were pushed by the Revolution into political activity. These petty bourgeois representatives of law and order, these opponents of "dictatorship," anarchy, and civil war, were not only eager supporters of the counter-revolutionary government of Ebert and Haase, but also had an essential ideological influence on the proletarian masses. Finally, there is the very crucial factor that, in this decisive struggle, the German working class lacked a genuine revolutionary vanguard party. The Spartacus League, persecuted by the government and the counter-revolution and fought with every means, was the heroically struggling front line of the German proletariat, but it was not an independent party and remained until December within the ranks of the USPD, as a result of its inconsistent attitude toward the question of party. But all the heroism of the Spartacists could not replace the strength of a genuine revolutionary vanguard party.

Because of these facts, the Revolution bogged down in the first stage, and then in the third stage, when the proletariat at last possessed a real class party and real guidance, through the founding of the KPD, it was robbed of its best leaders and finally struck down in bloody defeat.

Thus the November Revolution was, in character, a defeated proletarian revolution, one that did not move beyond its first beginnings.

II. COMMUNISM AND MILITARISM

The Communists Drove Ebert to the Military

KOPPEL S. PINSON

Did Ebert have any choice in facing the Communist threat but to call upon the professional soldiers of the old regime? The late Koppel S. Pinson argues that he did not, that Communist violence and insurrectionism drove him into the arms of the Supreme Command. If German militarism was thereby given new life, the Communists and not the Social Democrats should bear the blame. Lithuanian-born Pinson received his Ph.D. at Columbia and devoted his life to the study of nationalism, especially German nationalism. His textbook on German history, from which the present selection is taken, has become a standard reference for a whole generation of students. Pinson's spirited defense of Ebert reveals the chaotic conditions of the time and points up how difficult it would have been to forego the help of the old army.

THE SPARTACIST group had been formed in March, 1916, and it continued to work within the framework of the U.S.D.P. [Independent Social Democratic Party] during the last two years of the war. On December 14, 1918, it published its revolutionary program whereby it set itself apart from the U.S.D.P., and on December 29 to January 1 the organization meetings of the Communist party of Germany were held and the Spartacists formally seceded from the Independent Socialist party.

The leaders of the Spartacists were Karl Liebknecht and Rosa Luxemburg. Liebknecht, the son of the revered founder of the Social Democratic party, Wilhelm Liebknecht, became identified in the public eye with the fight against militarism and as the martyr for this cause. Not beloved in his own circles, he was possessed of great egotism, which was enormously inflated after he had been released from prison and hailed by cheering crowds as the martyred victim of Prussian militarism. But he was lacking in a sense of responsibility, and his intimate colleagues, well aware of this, had little faith in his political judgment.

Rosa Luxemburg, a Polish Jewess who had played a prominent role in the Polish Socialist movement before she came to Germany, was an intellectual giant compared to Liebknecht. But as Bernstein points out, "There stood before her eyes and lived in her soul an abstract conception of a proletariat that hardly corresponded to the real proletariat." There has been an attempt recently, especially by dissidents from the orthodox Communist party, to re-evaluate Rosa Luxemburg and to set her off from Lenin and the Russian Bolsheviks. Her essay on the Russian revolution, it is true, indicates a wavering feeling regarding the course of events under Lenin. And it is also true that she had greater intellectual acumen, a higher sense of personal integrity, and more political maturity than the band of youngsters who made up the bulk of the Spartacist group. But the basic lines of Spartacist policy, which were to be so fateful for the subsequent political situation in Germany, were laid down by her and bear the stamp of her personality and her ideas. A week after the outbreak of the revolution she wrote an article for *Die Rote Fahne* on "A Week of Revolution." Although the Hohenzollerns had been laid low, she declared, this was not of momentous consequence. For it was not the monarchy or the Hohenzollerns who were the real enemies and who had brought on the war. The monarchy was "like every bourgeois government, merely the business agent for the ruling classes." The real enemy was the imperialist-capitalist bourgeoisie. There could be no real revolution before it was eliminated, and "the future of the German revolution is anchored in the world revolution of the proletariat."

The Spartacists savagely attacked the Independents for entering into a partnership with the Majority Socialists. "Our first duty," declared Rosa Luxemburg before a Berlin meeting of the U.S.D.P., "is to destroy every bridge to the present government." The formal equality of democracy, she went on to say, "is nothing but lies and falsehoods so long as the economic power of capital still exists. . . . Socialism does not mean getting together in a parliament and deciding on laws. For us socialism means the smashing of the ruling classes with all the brutality that the proletariat is able to develop in its struggle." She further elaborated her conception of proletarian brutality in the *Rote Fahne* of December 14, 1918:

It is not when the wage slave and the capitalist, the agricultural proletarian and the Junker sit in sham equality to engage in parliamentary debates on their vital issues, that you have democracy; democracy that is not a swindle is to be found only when the million-headed proletarian masses seize the entire power of the state with their hardened fists in order, like the God Thor, to shatter the heads of the ruling classes with their hammer.

At the founding conference of the German Communist party Rosa Luxemburg delivered a long speech on "Our Program and the Political Situation." In it she called for a return to the Marxian doctrines of 1848 and a revision of the Socialist program which had existed up to August 4, 1914. Kautsky and the other party leaders, she said, had developed a parliamentary kind of Socialism which was a degeneration of Marxist theory. "The immediate task of the proletariat is none other than . . . to realize Socialism and to eradicate capitalism root and branch." This, she maintained against the majority of the delegates, cannot be carried out unless you have the masses behind you, including the peasantry. The masses must be educated and revolutionized to know what their duties are. But "the way to educate the masses to power is by letting them exercise power." And this is best achieved by strikes and civil war. The socialist revolution, she maintained, will come with a wave of strikes. Political strikes will become the central point of the revolution and put political action into a secondary role. "Civil war," she had written on November 20, "which they try to avoid with anxious care, does not allow itself to be eliminated. For civil war is only another name for class struggle, and the idea that you can introduce socialism without class struggle and by parliamentary majority decisions is a ludicrous petty-bourgeois illusion."

The Spartacist tactics and plan of action were, therefore, to undermine the existing government by all means possible, including armed insurrection. There was a division of opinion between Liebknecht and Luxemburg on the one hand, and the majority of the Spartacist following on the other, on the question of advisability of participating in the elections to the National Assembly. The party leaders urged participation because, they held, the tribune of the assembly could be utilized as a vehicle for revolutionary propaganda, but they were overruled by a vote of 62 to 32. But both factions agreed that "the chief action is to be on the streets" and not in the parliaments. The Ebert government was to be harassed and undermined at every step, and all means, including armed insurrection, were to be used to bring about its downfall. A Spartacist manifesto of December, 1918, proclaimed:

The rule of the working class is to be realized only through the path of an armed workers' revolution. The Communists are its vanguard. . . . The National Assembly that is being prepared by the present government will become an organ of the counter-revolutionists to crush the workers' revolution. All means must be used to prevent it from coming into being.

With a naïve belief that the process of history was working for them and that speedy world revolution was soon to be realized, the Spartacists began a policy of strikes, riots, street fighting, insurrections, which made the danger from the left the severest and most critical problem for the new revolutionary régime. This policy and tactics, incidentally, became the model for the strategy of the mass counter-revolution that later came from the right. The Spartacist tactics of revolt was a policy of catastrophe which drove the Majority Socialists into the arms of the reactionary militarists, which confused and divided the progressive elements of the population, which prevented the consolidation of democratic rule in republican Germany, and which contributed considerably to the brutalization of German political life.

The Spartacists represented at the time but a tiny fraction of the German workers. The great masses of the working population of the Reich were divided between the two other Socialist parties, with the Majority Socialists counting the largest following. But the Spartacists could always count on two things: (1) in a period of distress and want they could count on support from large elements of those disaffected at the time, and (2) they could always count on considerable support from the Independent Socialists. The U.S.D.P. in a sense bears the historical responsibility for making possible the growth and development of the Spartacists into the large Communist party of Germany. Had the Independents joined with the Majority Socialists to form one united party and had both groups carried out a decisive social and political policy, then one may safely say that the Spartacists would never have amounted to more than a tiny political faction. The ambiguous role of the U.S.D.P., and its constant attacks upon the government of the Majority Socialists, created an atmosphere favorable for the tactics of the Spartacists even in circles that were not Communist. Both the Spartacist policy of civil war and the Independents' equivocal position are revealed in the lamentable record of political strikes and armed insurrections that beset Germany between December, 1918, and June, 1919.

The disturbances, strikes, or insurrections, as the case may be, involved in some instances legitimate grievances, by sailors, soldiers, or workers. In almost all cases a large share of the violence was caused by undisciplined and irresponsible elements. Nor did the Majority Socialists do all they could to reassure the disaffected elements or the country at large of either resolute intention to carry out a plan of social and economic reform or of their complete break with the forces of the old order. But, with all that, it was the Spartacists who carried on agitation of the wildest character and favored a spirit of civil war, and it was the large elements of Independents and even bourgeois progressives who seemed to be engaged in rivalry with the Spartacists as to who was more revolutionary, and who gave them support in the cause of either world revolution or of social progress, who were chiefly to blame for the virtual civil war that began with the outbreak in Berlin on December 6 and continued throughout the Reich for the succeeding six months. Involved to a degree which cannot be established clearly and definitely, but the reality of which is indisputable, were also the support and help which came both from Bolshevik agents and from the Russian treasury.

Friday, December 6, 1918, was the first

of the "bloody days of the revolution." A minor action by rightist soldiers led to a counter mass demonstration by Spartacists, and ensuing excitement and bloodshed resulted in 16 dead and 12 seriously injured. A much more serious and violent outbreak occurred on December 23 and 24 when the sailors of the Volksmarine Division carried out a *Putsch,* occupied the Marstall and Schloss in the capital as well as the *Vorwärts* building, and held the Socialist commandant of Berlin, Otto Wels, as prisoner. This action led to several days of bloody fighting between the radicals and the government troops, caused death and serious injury to scores of persons and was the immediate cause for the resignation of the three Independent Socialist ministers from the government. Haase, Dittmann, and Barth were replaced by the Majority Socialists Noske and Rudolf Wissel, and the period of joint Socialist rule came to an end.

The tension between the Independent Socialist ministers and the Majority Socialists in the cabinet had been one of long standing. Their resignation from the cabinet on December 29th, for the alleged reason that they could not go along with the rest of the cabinet in sanctioning the "blood bath" of December 23–24, was only the climax of long-standing conflict. Haase and Barth have written that they were on the point of resigning on several occasions before this. The chief source of trouble revolved around the actions of the Majority Socialists in vesting too much confidence in the old military leaders and in the attempt made by the government to retain some of the old military divisions to fight against the Poles in the east and in the Baltic area against the Bolsheviks. The real trouble, however, was that the three U.S.D.P. ministers could never count on whole-hearted support for a policy of Socialist coalition within their own party. They were being continuously pressed to radical policies by the increased activities of Liebknecht and his followers, by the echo which these activities found in the left wing of the U.S.D.P., and by the continuous call for a break with the "traitors

to the revolution" and the "blood hounds." The resulting resignation of the Independent Socialist ministers was a serious blow to the revolution in that it weakened the new republic before the outside world by removing from power the very elements that stood for a complete break with imperial Germany. Internally it helped to increase the mistrust of the government by the more radical elements. It was, as Bernstein calls it, "a fatal capitulation before Spartacus."

The Spartacist uprising in January, 1919, has aptly been termed by Rudolf Hilferding the "Battle of the Marne" of the German revolution. It was more violent than any of the previous incidents, and also revealed more clearly than the others the patent political designs of the Spartacists. The ostensible cause of trouble in this instance revolved around the ouster of Emil Eichhorn, the police president of Berlin and a left-wing Independent. On January 3, the U.S.D.P. ministers in the Prussian government resigned from the cabinet, following the lead of their colleagues in the Reich cabinet. Eichhorn, anxious to retain hold of the key position as head of the police force in the capital, refused to leave his post. Called upon by Paul Hirsch, the Prussian minister of interior, to explain his obstructionist tactics or resign, Eichhorn declared that he had received his power from the revolution and would hold on to it in the interests of revolution. He was thereupon summarily dismissed by the Prussian government on January 4. This action aroused the heated passions of the left groups. The revolutionary shop stewards, the Berlin U.S.D.P., and the newly organized Communist party joined in a manifesto on January 5 which called the Berlin masses to a monster demonstration in the Siegesalee for that afternoon.

The official Communist party policy adopted at the time did not consider this to be the opportune time to overthrow the government. But at the meeting of the revolutionary shop stewards several reports were presented which claimed that strong military suport was available for the radicals. Liebknecht and Wilhelm Pieck thereupon came out for the overthrow of the Ebert-Scheidemann government. The majority voted to take up the struggle against the government until it was overthrown. A revolutionary committee of fifty-three was named, headed by Liebknecht, Ledebour, and Paul Scholze, and manifestoes were printed which proclaimed the overthrow of the government and the establishment of a new revolutionary government headed by the above three. The various newspaper buildings, including the *Vorwärts* building and other public buildings, were occupied by the insurgents. A general strike was proclaimed for January 6. The Majority Socialists countered with a call to their followers to a mass demonstration in the Wilhelmstrasse. Two rival mass demonstrations were thus going on simultaneously. From one side came the cries: "Down with Scheidemann! Down with Ebert! Long live the World Revolution!" The others shouted: "Down with Liebknecht! Down with Spartacus! Long live Democracy! Long live Socialism!" The Central Council of the Workers' and Soldiers' Councils called on all the councils to support the government, and the Executive of the Berlin Workers' Council voted 12 to 2 to support the ouster of Eichhorn. The moderate elements in the U.S.D.P. worked frantically to stop the fighting and restore unity, but to no avail.

The government demanded the full evacuation of all the occupied buildings, but the rebels stubbornly refused to give up the *Vorwärts* building. This was a challenge which no government, aiming not only to achieve stability at home but also engaged in delicate negotiations abroad, could afford to let go unanswered. The insurrection of the radicals had to be met with all the force the government could organize. What forces were there, however, that the government could muster? The tragedy of the German revolution lay in the fact that when the democratic elements of the revolution required the necessary force and power to give stability to their rule,

they found no such source of military power among their own worker supporters. The pacifist and anti-militarist tradition of the Socialist movement stood in the way of creating a strong republican military force to protect the new régime. After the resignation of the Independent Socialists from the cabinet, the three Majority Socialist ministers published the following plea to their supporters: "If you burden us with responsibility you must do more: You must create power for us! There can be no government without power! Without power we cannot carry out your mandate! . . . Do you want the German Socialist Republic? . . . Then help us create a people's force for the government that will be able to protect its dignity, its freedom of decision and its activity against assaults and putsches. . . . A government . . . that cannot assert itself has also no right to existence."

The response from the followers of the Majority Socialists and from the democratic bourgeoisie was weak and ineffectual. When military force was needed, the Majority Socialist government had to seek allies among the militarist circles of the old officer caste and the old army. The government decided to entrust Noske with the obligation to restore order. Noske, fully aware of the ominous character of his task, declared: "Someone must become the bloodhound! I cannot evade the responsibility." He became governor general of Berlin, and established his headquarters in Dahlem, a suburb of Berlin. He secured the co-operation of several old-régime generals — von Lüttwitz, von Wissel, von Roeder, von Maercker, von Hoffmann, and von Held — and recruited and drilled several thousand soldiers and officers. On the night of January 10 he marched on the center of the city. The buildings held by the rebels were stormed in several days of bitter fighting. The troops that rallied to the government were full of bitterness and scorn for the rebels and did not bother too often to discriminate between the different political tendencies. Indiscriminate shooting, brutality, and terrorization were practiced upon the prisoners. Even Karl Kautsky was arrested and held for several hours by a band of soldiers on the charge that he had once been in contact with Rosa Luxemburg. By January 13 the Communist revolt was completely suppressed. Ledebour and several other leaders of the rebels were arrested. Though Liebknecht and Rosa Luxemburg were able to hide out for several days, they were apprehended on the 15th of January. Liebknecht was shot "while trying to escape," and Luxemburg was brutally beaten down and her body thrown into the Landwehrkanal, from which it was not recovered until May 31.

*　*　*

The suppression of the insurrections in Bavaria, as well as in the rest of the Reich, by the alliance between the Majority Socialists and the old military groups has given rise to one of the most controversial problems in the story of the German revolution. The history of this alliance goes back to the working agreement between Ebert and General Groener, on November 9, 1918. The aim of this alliance, in the words of General Groener, "was to combat the revolution without reservation, to re-establish a lawful government, to lend this government armed support and to convene a National Assembly as soon as possible." General Groener, and other officers and military men who have presented their versions of this alliance, have always exhibited great glee in describing the dependence of the Socialists on the old officer caste, and they have no doubt exaggerated the character of the agreement.

Ebert's aim was not "to combat the revolution" but to combat Bolshevism. But in pursuing this aim Ebert and Noske came to rely heavily on the old-line soldiers. There had always been a direct secret telephone connection between the chancellor's office and the office of the Supreme Command. When Ebert moved into the chancellery he used this line to confer with Groener every evening. Whether this meant, as Volkmann describes it, that "Ebert took off the

iron mask he carried all day, opened up to Groener and received from him encouragement and comfort," and, as Emil Barth describes him, that he came back to the cabinet meetings more cocky and self-assured after these secret conversations, is difficult to establish. The private line was most convenient to Ebert and his colleagues on December 23, when they were locked up by the revolt of the sailors and this was the only way in which Ebert was able to summon help for the government.

Be that as it may, Ebert and Noske came to rely for the support of the government upon the monarchist soldiers and officers who were interested not in saving the republic but in preserving a military framework on which to create a revived military machine in the future. The chaotic conditions in the east and in the Baltic, where Polish and German nationalism confronted each other and where the armed struggle against Bolshevist troops was carried on, led also to the organization of various types of military formations. These volunteer corps, or *Freikorps,* became the centers for military adventurers, reactionary officers, chauvinist nationalists, and designing generals who laid their plans for a future comeback. Organized to protect the revolution against insurrection from the left, they became the spearheads of the counter-revolution and the sources from which came eventually the gravediggers of the Weimar Republic. Ebert, Noske, and the Majority Socialists certainly did not have this ultimate objective in mind. Nor did they realize the brutalities and terroristic acts committed by many of these officers. They were horrified by the brutal murder of Liebknecht and Luxemburg and by the assassination of Eisner. They branded publicly these incidents as "acts of lynch justice" which "disgrace the German people" and "to be morally condemned by everyone, no matter on what side he may be." Noske frankly admitted that his government troops had been guilty of excesses. Nor can it be said that Noske exulted in his sense of military power. Every act of repression that he ordered was forced upon him by a putschist or insurrectionary act of the Spartacists. He spurned all overtures made to him from various channels to become "the man of the hour" and make himself military dictator. What he did was always carried out on instructions from and with the consent of the government.

The Majority Socialists, however, were still so much the "prisoners of August 4" that they were not sufficiently sensitive to the grave dangers of an alliance with the militarists. Their national patriotism was so embedded in their consciousness that it led them to place far too great trust in the old generals, and not only to use them for the necessary purposes of the government but also to give them credit for purer motives and higher ideals than they merited. It was this unrealistic appraisal of the continued *esprit de corps* of the officer caste that led the Socialists to turn over the murderers of Liebknecht and Luxemburg to be tried by their own fellow officers and as a result to get off with light sentences and then be aided to escape. Similar incidents occurred with the murderers of Gustav Landauer and other radicals. This only caused further intensification of the mistrust of the new government by anti-militarist circles at home and by public opinion abroad.

* * *

Due recognition must be given to the Social Democrats of Germany for having saved not only Germany but all of Europe from the very real threat of Communist world revolution that hovered over Europe in the first years of the republic.

The Communists Not Guilty

ERIC WALDMAN

Eric Waldman, now a professor of political science at the University of Calgary, served as an American army operations officer in occupied Germany from 1945 to 1949 and has maintained a continuing interest in German affairs. After a careful and unusually dispassionate reassessment of the German Communists' ideology, strength, and behavior in 1918–1919, Waldman concludes that they had neither the capability nor the immediate intention of overthrowing the Ebert government and were not primarily responsible for the ill-fated January uprising. These questions are important because the reader's judgment about the crucial issue of the military may well depend on whether he finds Waldman or the previous writer, Pinson, more convincing concerning the danger of Communism.

IN SPITE of the Spartacists' violent opposition to any action directed toward a consolidation of the unfinished revolution, they did not plan, prepare, or organize an armed uprising with the intention of overthrowing the government — regardless of the many allegations of their numerous contemporary enemies. Neither their political utterances and written statements nor their actions can be used to support these claims which were widely disseminated not only by "bourgeois" and military circles but also by the Majority Socialists. In fact, both the political concepts and the actions of the Spartacists at that time followed a very simple and open pattern which does not resemble the deceptive tactics of contemporary Communist parties.

Their short-range revolutionary tactics were based on the following assumptions: (1) the revolution was being betrayed by the Majority Socialists who were supported in their endeavors by the traditional enemies of political, social, and economic progress; (2) most of the workers were unaware of the course which developments took after the mass uprising of November and, therefore, could not understand the "treacher-ous" action of the SPD and of the moderate wing of the USPD.

The Spartacists' conviction of the political immaturity of the workers and soldiers did not affect their confidence in the masses. It was merely a statement of fact which called for specific remedies. Revolutionary propaganda and "revolutionary actions" were the means by which the Spartacists intended to educate the masses and gradually win over the majority of the working class. The revolutionary actions referred to were nothing more than street demonstrations and strikes, primarily of a political nature. Because of their political content, leading inevitably to clashes with the "reactionary" forces of the government, they would attract more and more workers and revolutionize growing segments of the masses. It was nothing but an extension of the old "revolutionary gymnastics," as the opponents of the Spartacists called Liebknecht's tactics before and during the November uprising.

While Liebknecht tended more toward action, Rosa Luxemburg believed that the principal mission of the Spartacist League was "to arouse a socialist spirit and con-

From Eric Waldman, *The Spartacist Uprising of 1919*, Marquette German Studies, I (Milwaukee, 1958), pp. 127–33, 157, 184–92. Reprinted by permission of The Marquette University Press.

sciousness in the workers." However, both apparently agreed that the proletarian revolution was only the beginning of a long and tedious road, and both — but particularly Rosa Luxemburg — warned their followers against rash actions. As late as December 23, 1918, after numerous armed clashes between left wing radicals and various other groups, including military formations — struggles which often were used to illustrate the allegation that the Spartacists wanted to overthrow the government by a putsch — Liebknecht declared in a speech in Berlin:

At present the Spartacists are attacked from all sides. The newspapers of the bourgeoisie and the social patriots, from the *Vorwaerts* to the *Kreuzzeitung,* abound with the most fantastic lies, with the most insolent misrepresentations, with distortions, and defamations. There is nothing we are not accused of. We are supposed to advocate terror; we are presumed to intend to start the bloodiest civil war; we are presumed to have equipped ourselves with weapons and ammunition in preparation for the armed revolt.

The Spartacists remained confident throughout the consolidation phase that, as long as the workers could prevent the counter-revolutionary forces from suppressing the revolutionary movement, the masses eventually would follow the political program of the Spartacist League. Their confidence in the masses received new impetus when the huge strike movement was started at the end of November 1918 by the metal workers in Berlin and the miners in Upper Silesia and the Ruhr area. The strikes spread rapidly to other industries throughout Germany and involved great numbers of workers. The workers originally struck for purely economic reasons but soon political demands came into play. Clashes with counterrevolutionary troops resulted in the death of many workers. The Spartacists interpreted the spontaneous mass strikes as an indication that the workers again were beginning to take matters into their own

hands in spite of the efforts of the consolidation forces. Rosa Luxemburg believed that these strikes would grow in size and importance and would become the focal points of the revolution. She also predicted that the revolution would assume an economic character and would become a truly socialist revolution.

In an article in *Die Rote Fahne* she greeted these strikes as the beginning of the most powerful phase of direct mass action:

Instead of waiting for the blessed decrees of the government or for the decisions of the famous national assembly, the masses instinctively reach for the only real means which leads to socialism: *the fight against capital.* Up to now, the government has exerted every effort to castrate the revolution and to establish harmony among classes. . . .

The proletarian masses upset . . . the revolutionary class harmony and wave the dreaded banner of the class struggle.

The growing strike movement is proof that the political revolution invaded the social foundation of society. The revolution recalls its own original cause; it puts aside the paper wing of personnel changes and decrees which did not in the slightest effect changes in the social relation between capital and labor, and places itself upon the stage of events.

* * *

The strikes which have just broken out are within [the framework] of the present revolution, and are not controversies of a "trade-union type" pertaining to trifles, to wage problems. They are the masses' natural answer to the powerful shock which capitalism has experienced as the result of the breakdown of German imperialism and the short political revolution of the workers and soldiers. They are the first beginning of a complete settlement between capital and labor in Germany; they introduce the start of a powerful, direct [form of] class struggle in which the outcome can be nothing other than the removal of the capitalist wage system and the introduction of the socialist economy. They release the active social power of the present revolution: the revolutionary class energy of the proletarian masses. They open up the period of direct activity on the part of the great masses.

This interpretation of the strike movement by Rosa Luxemburg was later strongly criticized by the representatives of the official Communist creed because, according to them, it revealed once more her two greatest weaknesses: over-confidence in the spontaneity of the masses, and lack of appreciation of the role of a revolutionary class party. By the middle of December 1918, however, there were already specific signs that the need for a proletarian party which could supply leadership to the revolutionary masses was increasingly recognized by many of the Spartacists and other left wing radicals.

It is possible to see in Rosa Luxemburg's program for the Spartacist League — published on December 14, 1918, in *Die Rote Fahne* — a conscious step toward uniting the left wing radicals by providing them with a common platform. Considering that it preceded the founding of the KPD by only two weeks and the so-called "Spartacist Uprising" by about three weeks, this comprehensive statement of the Spartacists' political concepts and policies was important for several reasons. First of all, the program re-emphasized the ideological independence of the Spartacists from major Leninist concepts by specifically rejecting the use of terror as a tactical method and the precept of dictatorship by a minority. Secondly, it clarified the position of the Spartacists *vis-à-vis* the Ebert government and any other "bourgeois" government, as a policy of non-participation and non-interference in governmental affairs until the Spartacist League had the support of the majority of the proletariat. Thirdly, it formulated tactics for the long period of class struggle aimed at securing the confidence and support of the masses. Fourthly, it provided the basis for searching discussions among the left wing radicals during the two weeks which intervened between the announcement of the program and the founding of the KPD.

Rosa Luxemburg's clear formulation of these political concepts left no room for misinterpretations, especially of those issues related to the Spartacists' position toward a *coup d'état.* Her statement concerning the rejection of terror reads as follows:

The proletarian revolution requires no terror methods [to realize] its objectives; it hates and despises violence and murder. It does not require this means of combat because it does not fight against individuals but against institutions. . . . It is not a desperate attempt of a minority to shape the world by force according to its ideals, but the action of great masses of people who are called up to fulfill a historic mission and to transform historic necessity into reality.

In the conclusions to the program, Rosa Luxemburg summarized the position of the Spartacist League as follows:

The Spartacist League is not a party desirous of obtaining political power over the working masses or through the working masses.

The Spartacist League is only the most conscious part of the proletariat [in terms of] objectives, pointing incessantly to the historic task for the entire broad masses of the working class, representing throughout the individual phases of the revolution the ultimate socialist objective and representing in all national issues the interests of the proletarian world revolution.

The Spartacist League rejects the idea of sharing power with Scheidemann and Ebert, tools of the bourgeoisie, because in this type of collaboration, it sees treason to the fundamentals of socialism, strengthening of the counterrevolution, and paralysis of the revolution.

The Spartacist League will never assume governmental power unless it is supported by the clear, decisive will of the great majority of the proletariat in Germany, and in no other way except with their conscious acceptance of the ideas, objectives, and fighting methods of the Spartacist League. . . .

The KPD had only a few thousand members throughout Germany. In Berlin there were barely fifty members. It was an elite party or the framework for a mass party which remained isolated from the socialist masses for a considerable time. . . .

A factual evaluation of the January events supports the assertion that the "Spartacist Uprising" was not a premeditated undertaking but was an outgrowth of the policy meeting of January 5 held by the left wing factions because of the overwhelming mass response to the Eichhorn incident. The estimate of the revolutionary situation arrived at by the over-optimistic radical leaders — especially concerning the attitude of the soldiers — was incorrect and misleading. However, there is general agreement among contemporaneous observers that a determined leadership could have seized political power in Berlin either on January 5 or 6. How long the revolutionaries could have retained power is another question; it appears that, since the rest of Germany would not have followed the example set in the capital, it would have been only a short "council dictatorship." Because the Revolutionary Committee was divided internally concerning its own objectives, it was incapable of giving directives to the masses which waited patiently for two days. The Revolutionary Committee decided to maintain the occupation of strategically and tactically unimportant buildings instead of seizing the traditional seats of political power, such as the Chancellery and the Ministry of War. In this context it really did not matter if those buildings were originally occupied by spontaneous mass actions or through the agitation of *agents provocateurs*.

An examination of the events leading to the January fighting does not support the assertion that the SPD government provoked the action of the left wing radicals in order to create a situation in which the government would be justified in suppressing by force. It was not the beginning of a contemplated all-out offensive by the government against the opposition forces. However, once the position of power began to change in favor of the government, the

determination to settle the basic issue with the revolutionary trouble-makers won the upper hand.

The number of persons killed during the January uprising remains unknown. Even reliable estimates are not available.

* * *

The attitude of the Communists toward the uprising was not uniform. Their views toward an expansion of the mass protest demonstration on behalf of Eichhorn into a full-scale fight for the seizure of political power were divided as follows: (1) Karl Liebknecht and Wilhelm Pieck, the two Central Committee members who participated in the January 5 meeting of the functionaries of the Revolutionary Shop Stewards and of the Berlin USPD, strongly endorsed the uprising. (2) Rosa Luxemburg, Leo Jogiches, and the rest of the Central Committee of the KPD were opposed but believed that, regardless of their views, the new KPD had the moral obligation to support the revolutionary workers in their life and death struggle. (3) Karl Radek was strictly opposed to the uprising and urgently advocated discontinuing the hopeless fight before the revolutionary organizations suffered severe defeats which would affect their work for a long time to come.

Liebknecht and Pieck, in siding with the advocates of the uprising, had acted without the knowledge and approval of the Central Committee of the KPD. Liebknicht was severely criticized by Rosa Luxemburg for his unilateral action. How many of the rank and file members of the Spartacists concurred with Liebknecht's endorsement of the all-out struggle for power is not known. During the days of the uprising, Liebknecht spent his time either in conferences with the Revolutionary Committee or with the dispersed groups of entrenched insurgents. He maintained little contact with the party leadership. On January 10, the Central Committee finally ordered Liebknecht and Pieck not to continue their participation in the Revolutionary Committee. This directive was meaningless by then since the committee had already suspended its meetings and had scattered in all directions.

The attitude of most of the KPD leaders, including Rosa Luxemburg and Leo Jogiches, toward the uprising was determined by their conviction that political developments in Germany had not reached the point where an attempt to assume power should be made. The decision of the January 5 meeting in favor of the all-out fight created a difficult problem for the Communist leaders. Should the KPD support the fight of the revolutionary workers in spite of the fact that the Central Committee did not endorse the uprising and was certain from the beginning that the insurrection had no real chance of realizing its objectives? Rosa Luxemburg's views (which doubtlessly reflected the Party's position on this controversial issue) were related by Clara Zetkin on the basis of a letter she had received from Leo Jogiches, who probably was Rosa Luxemburg's closest collaborator during the January days.

Rosa Luxemburg saw the events — as significant and as hopeful as they were — not from the viewpoint of the assault against the Berlin City Hall. She related these events to the prevailing situation and especially to the degree of political maturity of the broad population of all Germany. On that basis, the overthrow of the Ebert government could be, for the time-being, only a propagandistic over-all slogan of the revolutionary proletarians, and not the immediate objective of revolutionary struggles. Under the prevailing circumstances related primarily to Berlin, in the most favorable case they [the revolutionary fighters] could have led to a Berlin "Commune," . . . The aim of the fight could only be a strong defense against the attack of the counterrevolution. Thus the reinstatement of Eichhorn, the withdrawal of the troops which were to subjugate the revolutionary proletariat of Berlin in a violent manner, the arming of the workers, and the transfer of the military command power to the revolutionary political representatives of the proletarians — these

were the demands which required action, not negotiations.

Because of this situation, the young Communist Party led by Rosa Luxemburg had a difficult mission, full of conflicts. It could not accept the objective of the mass action — the overthrow of the government; it had to reject this aim, but at the same time it was not permitted to detach itself from the masses which had taken up the fight. In spite of this contradiction the Party had to remain with the masses; it had to remain among the masses to strengthen the fighters in their struggle against the counter-revolution and to expedite the process of their revolutionary maturation during the operations by making them aware of the purpose of their struggle. Toward this end, the Communist Party had to reveal its own aims and make known its precise estimate of the situation without injuring the revolutionary solidarity it owed to the fighters. . . .

Thus the Communists joined the insurgents not because they believed that the uprising was a politically and tactically well-founded operation, but because of the obligation the Party thought it owed to the revolutionary fighters. "Under the circumstances there was only one decision possible for the Communist Party: to remain with the fighters, to strengthen their power of resistance and their courage, to be ready not only to share in their victories but also in their defeats." The KPD also intended to aid the revolutionary mass action by clarifying and limiting objectives. The aims set by the Communists for the uprising were disarmament of the counterrevolution, arming of the proletariat, merger of all revolutionary troops into a Red Guard, and new elections for the workers' and soldiers' councils in order to bring their composition into harmony with the changes which had occurred since November, 1918. The overthrow of the Ebert government, the main purpose of the uprising as determined by the Revolutionary Committee, became the slogan and general directive for the entire coming phase of the revolution.

The articles of Rosa Luxemburg, "What Are the Leaders Doing?" and "Neglected Duties," in *Die Rote Fahne* present a candid view of the KPD about the revolutionary implications of the January Uprising. They also furnish an insight into Communist attempts to formulate limited and reasonable objectives and to compel the revolutionary leaders of the insurrection to fulfill their obligations.

Those who saw yesterday's [January 6, 1919] mass demonstrations in the Siegesallee, who felt this adamant revolutionary conviction, this magnificent attitude, this energy flowing from the masses, must have reached the [following] conclusions: the proletarians have grown enormously in a political sense through the experience of the last weeks. They have realized their strength and lack nothing but to use their power.

However, have their leaders, the executive organs of their will, progressed with them? Have the Revolutionary Shop Stewards and Confidence Men of the large factories, have the radical elements of the USP acquired more energy and more determination in the meantime? Has their capacity for action kept abreast of the growing energy of the masses?
. . . The masses followed the call of their leaders with impetuosity. . . . They are waiting for further directives and actions from their leaders.

What have the leaders done in the meantime, what have they decided? What measures have they taken to secure the victory of the revolution in this tense situation during which the fate of the revolution will be decided at least for the next phase? We see and hear nothing! It may be true that the representatives of the working class are thoroughly and abundantly *conferring*. However, now is the time to *act*.

No time must be wasted. Thorough measures must be taken immediately. Clear and urgent directives must be given to the masses and to the soldiers who remained faithful to the cause of the revolution; . . .

Act! Act! Courageously, decisively, and constantly — that is the . . . duty and obligation of the Revolutionary Shop Stewards and of the honest socialist party leaders. Disarm the counterrevolution, arm the masses, and occupy all positions of power. Act quickly! . . .
. . . The weakness and immaturity of the revolution manifest themselves in the questions: *How* does one conduct the fight to re-

move the Ebert government? *How* does one convert this increased internal maturity into practical use? Nothing like the last three days have shown so strongly these weaknesses and deficiencies.

The elimination of the Ebert-Scheidemann government does not mean storming into the palace of the Reich Chancellery and chasing away or arresting a few people: it means first of all to seize all real power positions and *hold on* to them and *make use* of them.

The experience of the last three days speaks eloquently to the leaders of the working class: Do not talk! Do not confer forever! Do not negotiate! *Act*.

Karl Radek's opposition to the January uprising and to the participation of the KPD in the futile attempt to seize political power cannot be accepted as an indication of the official Soviet attitude toward the events. It is highly doubtful that Radek had any contact with his party during this period. His views are of great interest because they can be cited as proof that the Bolsheviks did not incite the German revolutionary leaders to the uprising contrary to the assertions of Edward Bernstein. On the basis of the information available to this writer, at the beginning of January, Radek was the only official representative of the Bolsheviks in Berlin. As has been said, he shared the belief of Rosa Luxemburg and her associates that the time for the all-out struggle for power had not yet come. He added authority to this conviction because of his reputation among the Communists as an experienced revolutionary tactician. On January 6, he declared his opposition to the decision of the January 5 meeting. On the 9th, he addressed a letter to the Central Committee of the KPD in which he requested that the Party use its influence upon the Revolutionary Committee and the proletarian masses to cease the insurrection immediately. He offered the following reasons for his request:

In your program pamphlet, "What Does the Spartacist League Want?", you explain that you intend to take over the government only when you have the majority of the working class behind you. This absolutely correct stand finds its justification in the simple fact that a government of the workers is unthinkable without an existing proletarian mass organization. At present, the only mass organizations to be considered, the workers' and soldiers' councils, are of only nominal strength. . . . In this situation, one cannot even consider the proletariat's taking over political power. If the government should fall into your hands as the result of a *coup d'état,* within a few days it would be cut off from the rest of the country and would be strangled.

In this situation, the action taken by the Revolutionary Shop Stewards in response to the attack of the social-patriotic government against the police headquarters, should have been only a protest action. The advance guard of the proletariat — provoked by government policy and misled by the Revolutionary Shop Stewards, who as the result of their political inexperience are not capable of understanding the power relation throughout the entire Reich — has in its enthusiasm transformed the protest demonstration into a struggle for political power. This enables Ebert and Scheidemann to strike a blow against the Berlin movement which can weaken the entire movement for months. The only force which can prevent this disaster is you, the Communist Party. You have sufficient insight to know that the fight is hopeless; . . . Nothing can prevent a weaker [power] from retreating before a superior force.

Shortly after the last skirmishes ended, Rosa Luxemburg evaluated the events of Spartacus Week. In her article "Order Rules in Berlin" (*Die Ordnung herrscht in Berlin*), she explained that a victory of the proletarians — the overthrow of the Ebert government and the establishment of a socialist dictatorship — could not be expected because of the political immaturity of the German Revolution. The fact that the soldiers, most of whom were from rural areas which were hardly affected by the

revolution, could be used for suppressing the revolutionary workers was for Rosa Luxemburg one of the significant symptoms of the general political immaturity of Germany. Under these circumstances a victory of the working class was impossible.

. . . A final and lasting victory in this moment could not be expected. Was, therefore, the fight of the last week a "mistake"? Yes, if it had been an intentional "assault," a so-called "putsch." However, what was the cause of the fighting of the past week? As in all previous instances . . . it was a brutal provocation of the government! . . . The revolutionary working class was *forced* to take up arms. It was a *matter of revolutionary honor* to repel immediately the assault of the [counterrevolution]. . . .

Rosa Luxemburg emphasized that the suppression of the January Uprising was only a defeat in one single engagement, and she predicted that the next day the revolution would proclaim: "I was, I am, I shall be!"

Liebknecht was of the same mind. The uprising was defeated because "the time was not ripe" for it. This could not be helped because the workers had not chosen to start the fight. "The fight was forced on the proletariat by the Ebert-gang."

Indeed, it was a strange twist of history which gave the January Uprising the name of that left wing opposition group within the German socialist movement which officially had nothing to do with starting the insurrection and which became connected with it only to maintain "proletarian solidarity." If the January Uprising must be identified at all with a left-wing faction, then the Revolutionary Shop Stewards, whose functionaries voted unanimously for it, should be first in line for this "honor."

Militarism's New Lease on Life

S. WILLIAM HALPERIN

Americans have generally been hostile to the anti-democratic forces of traditional conservatism in Germany, and especially to the army. It is not surprising, then, that the dominant current of American historiography finds fault with the Social Democrats for allying themselves with the old army and shortsightedly entrusting the defense of the new democracy to the most profoundly anti-democratic institution of the old regime. The respected University of Chicago historian, S. William Halperin, expresses this widespread opinion in his early and classic political history of the Weimar Republic, *Germany Tried Democracy*. The crucial question is whether the Social Democratic leaders had any other choice. The belief that they did, that they might have disbanded the old army and created a pro-republican militia to defend their government, forms part of the "Third Way" viewpoint that will receive further scrutiny in Part III.

THE SOCIAL DEMOCRATS had no armed force of their own with which to suppress the radicals. So Ebert turned to the Supreme Command. He did so in the belief that an understanding with the army leaders was the only way to save the country from Bolshevism and civil war. He got in touch by telephone with general headquarters at Spa. His party comrades were unaware of his action. Groener proved receptive. He was strongly of the opinion that the officers' corps should conclude an alliance with the Social Democrats who, after all, were moderates. The purpose of this alliance was to be twofold: to preserve the position and power of the military caste and combat the extreme Left. The monarchy, Groener felt, could not be restored. Consequently, the officers would have to make the best of the existing situation; and this they could do by assenting to a deal with Ebert. Groener had little difficulty in persuading Hindenburg to go along. The advantages which would accrue to the military caste were obvious. Besides, the field marshal, like his First Quartermaster General, detested the newly formed workers' and soldiers' councils and yearned to see them abolished. In such an enterprise, the Social Democrats would prove indispensable allies. Groener informed Ebert that Hindenburg was prepared to remain at the head of the Supreme Command. In return, the government would have to support the officers' corps.

In this fashion did the famous Ebert-Groener deal of November 10, 1918, come into being. Its importance can scarcely be exaggerated. Backed by the regular army, the Social Democrats were now in a position to suppress the radicals. The doom of German Bolshevism was apparently sealed. The old-line generals, who deeply regretted the overthrow of the monarchy, retained their powers and functions. Control of the nation's armed forces remained in their hands. This was one of the reasons why the Social Democrats never seriously attempted to create a republican army. Their alliance with the Supreme Command robbed them of freedom of action. The work of making the new Germany safe for militarism, whose destruction had been one of the principal aims of the revolution, was thus begun on November 10, 1918.

* * *

From S. William Halperin, *Germany Tried Democracy* (New York, 1946), pp. 99–100, 114–16, 105–07. Reprinted by permission of the Thomas Y. Crowell Company.

On December 16, 1918, the delegates [to the National Congress of Councils] assembled in the Prussian House of Deputies for the opening session. A great crowd, palpably under radical leadership, besieged the building and demonstrated noisily in an effort to influence the proceedings. From the very beginning, however, it was manifest that the extremists had grievously miscalculated. Not they but the Social Democrats, the alleged betrayers of the revolution, enjoyed the support of the great majority of the delegates. Liebknecht and Luxemburg received a resounding rebuff straightway when the assembly voted overwhelmingly against giving them seats. Richard Mueller, the leader of the Shop Stewards, started the verbal fireworks by denouncing the Haase-Dittmann policy of co-operating with the Social Democrats. While he was speaking, a Spartacist delegation forced its way into the hall and demanded the removal of the Ebert government, the transfer of supreme power to the workers' and soldiers' councils, the formation of a Red army and the issuance of a call for world revolution. This incursion was but the first of a whole series of interruptions which kept the congress in a continuous state of turmoil. On the following day, the bitterness between the Social Democrats and the radicals flared anew. Lebedour denounced Ebert in excoriating terms. But it was Barth who cause the greatest stir. He declared that his patience was at an end. He would have to decide very soon whether he wished to remain a member of the government. He had vainly combated Ebert's policies. He could no longer assume any responsibility for them. He wanted an immediate understanding with the Russians. The military "camarilla," he warned, was at work against the new regime and was being clandestinely supported by the Social Democrats. This situation must not be tolerated another moment. The time to do away with the old officers' corps was now.

Ebert reacted sharply to the charge that he had established treasonable relations with the generals. He told the congress that the questions raised by Barth were not the kind that could be settled by public debate. Haase intervened at this point. He was anxious to prevent a widening of the breach between Ebert and the Independents. Consequently he suggested that action be delayed on Barth's demand for abolition of the officers' corps. The proceedings were suddenly interrupted by the arrival of a delegation of soldiers. Dorrenbach, head of the People's Naval Division, led the intruders. He demanded that the officers be disarmed, that all rank insignia be abolished, and that control of the armed forces be entrusted to a council of soldiers. He and his comrades clamored for immediate action and showed not the slightest intention of leaving until their demands had been granted. So great was the ensuing tumult that the congress was forced to suspend its labors. When it reconvened on the morning of December 18, an unexpected development occurred. Walther Lampl, the Social Democratic delegate from Hamburg, made common cause with Dorrenbach. Declaring that the time for action had come, he proceeded to introduce a number of sweeping motions. First and foremost on the list of his demands was the transfer of the powers of the Supreme Command to the cabinet and the executive committee of the workers' and soldiers' councils. He likewise insisted upon the elimination of all rank insignia, the election of officers by the soldiers themselves, the abolition of the standing army and the speedy creation of a people's militia. The friendly reception accorded Lampl's motions was a heavy blow to Ebert and to the program which he and Groener had clandestinely agreed upon. Ebert's plan to use the army to suppress left-wing radicalism would obviously come to nought if Hindenburg and Groener were denuded of their powers as top-ranking members of the Supreme Command. Such a possibility now seemed in the offing. For the fear of a militarist counterrevolution was no longer confined to the radicals; it had taken hold of important sections of the Social Democratic party. Lampl's motions were adopted by an overwhelming majority. Ebert's attempt to emasculate them by the addition of qualifying clauses proved vain. For the first time since proclamation of the republic, the three proletarian parties stood shoulder to shoulder. But the action of the congress changed nothing. Ebert saw to that. Thanks to him, control of the army remained in the hands of Hindenburg and Groener. And nothing was done to implement the other resolutions. German militarism was saved from what might have been a crippling blow.

* * *

Almost on the very morrow of the armistice, German militarists, reinforced by right-wing politicians and publicists, disseminated far and wide the theory that the armies of the Reich had never been defeated on the battlefield, that they had been stabbed in the back by "subversive" elements at home — pacifists, liberals, socialists, communists, Jews. Hindenburg made himself a leading exponent of this theory. In the last chapter of his memoirs, which appeared in September, 1919, he wrote: "Like Siegfried, stricken down by the treacherous spear of savage Hagen, our weary front collapsed." A few months later he made the same point before a Reichstag committee investigating the causes of Germany's collapse.

In spite of the superiority of the enemy in men and material, we could have brought the struggle to a favorable issue if determined and unanimous cooperation had existed between the army and those at home. But . . . divergent interests began to manifest themselves with us. These circumstances soon led to a disintegration of our will to conquer. . . .

This charge was taken up by Hitler and countless other propagandists.

The theory of the stab in the back proved a source of endless tribulation for the German republic. Its corollary, the myth of victory in the field, helped to preserve the prestige of the army. Between them they lent powerful impetus to the resurgence of militarism in Germany.

The leaders of the republic completed the work of making Germany safe for militarism. On November 10, 1918, they had thrown away their opportunity to create a people's army upon which they could have relied to checkmate the counterrevolutionists. Their behavior thereafter was of a piece with this initial capitulation. They shrank from performing the drastic economic and social operations which might have prevented the restoration of anything resembling the pre-1918 order. Generals who did not even bother to disguise their hostility to the democratic regime were permitted to retain important commands. The Reichswehr, that small but beautifully trained army of the German republic, was placed under the direction of men who had only contempt for their civilian superiors. The indoctrination to which the soldiers were subjected stressed the virtues and values of the old imperial army. They were made to feel that their first allegiance was to their military superiors and not to the regime which they had sworn to uphold. Through their control of the armed forces, the Reichswehr chieftains eventually became one of the most powerful groups in the country.

The goal of the military caste was to make possible the establishment of a regime which would do its will, which would dedicate the resources of the state to war and conquest. An essential preliminary to the achievement of this goal was the destruction or emasculation of democracy at home. As the star of the dethroned Hohenzollerns declined, most of the officers cold-storaged their traditional monarchism. They lent their support to any movement or party which gave promise of being strong enough to carry out their program. They even stooped to dealings with low-born demagogues whom they secretly despised. In the end it was Hitler, a man far removed from their own antecedents and social milieu, who gave them what they wanted.

The 27th of November, 1918, witnessed the forging of another important link in the chain of events that made possible the comeback of the military caste. On that day the Supreme Command took action to reinforce, by means of voluntary enlistment, the armed forces of the nation that were being depleted at a great rate in response to the widespread demand for instantaneous demobilization. The formation of fighting units composed exclusively of volunteers proceeded rapidly. Within a few weeks such units were to be found in every part of the Reich. Some of them helped the police to maintain order at home. Others were active along the eastern frontier and especially in the Baltic provinces. Still others were used to bolster detachments of the regular army. This influx of volunteers into the armed forces wes encouraged by the Social Democratic members of the government. At the behest of the Supreme Command, they issued a call for new recruits. They wished to have at their disposal a large military force that could be used against the Independents and the Spartacists. It was thus that the notorious Free Corps came into being. They were made up for the most part of professional soldiers and officers. These men were fanatically anti-Bolshevist, anti-socialist and anti-democratic. They hated the republic and everything it signified. They glorified militarism and the leadership principle. They were eager to fight for the restoration of the old order. Little wonder, then, that the Free Corps served as the spearhead of the counterrevolutionary forces during the first and crucial years of the German republic.

III. WAS THERE A THIRD WAY?

Social Revolution to Guarantee Democracy

ARTHUR ROSENBERG

The controversy over the military problem can serve to introduce the broader question of whether a "Third Way" existed for Germany in 1918 between Russian-style Communism and the fateful compromises of the Weimar Republic. Third Way advocates contend that the political democratization of Germany could not be secure unless a genuine social revolution destroyed the power of the old authoritarian establishment. Social Democratic leaders, instead of tying themselves to the old army and bureaucracy (those twin pillars of Prussian authoritarianism), should have created their own militia and transformed the councils into permanent instruments of democratic administration. Instead of leaving the great industrialists and Junker landowners in command of the economy, they should have socialized large-scale industry and broken up the Junker estates. Arthur Rosenberg provides the classic exposition of the Third Way viewpoint. Trained as an ancient historian and holding a position at the University of Berlin, Rosenberg was politically activated by the November Revolution: he joined the USPD and a little later the KPD, eventually serving as a Communist Reichstag deputy. But by 1927 he had broken with the party —now Stalinist controlled—and his numerous historical works (including this one, written in exile in 1935) testify convincingly that his commitment to democracy was no less deep than his commitment to socialism.

THE LOSERS in the November Revolution were the supporters of the old Prussian feudal system — the officers, landed gentry, and high government officials. In those days they felt themselves to be completely powerless. The officers continued to perform their duties by permission of the Government and the Soldiers' Councils. This was also true of the higher officials who had remained at their posts. The great landowners east of the Elbe anxiously awaited a future that seemed likely to bring with it the confiscation of their estates. In those days the Prussian Junker was powerless to offer armed resistance to any such action. The Lutheran peasantry who had been the support of the Conservatives until the outbreak of war, were embittered by bureaucratic maladministration of wartime food supplies, and, above all, by the sacrifice of blood and money that had been demanded of them during four long years of war. The peasant desired peace, and had lost all interest for and sympathy with the former system of government. This was shown by the course of events during the military revolts in the early days of November, when not a single body of troops recruited from the peasantry set itself in opposition to the Revolution. It is true that these peasants were very far from being Socialists. Nevertheless the new

From Arthur Rosenberg, *A History of the German Republic* (London, 1936), pp. 5–6, 21–27, 44–47. Translated by Ian F. D. Morrow and L. Marie Sieveking. Reprinted by permission of Methuen & Co., Ltd.

Government had nothing to fear from them, especially if it expropriated and divided up among them the great East Elbian estates, and gave the land that had formerly belonged to the noblemen to the small peasant and the agricultural labourer.

The great industrialists were no less powerless than the feudal nobles who had governed Germany until October, 1918. The State authority that had hitherto protected them with a powerful hand against the demands of the workmen no longer existed. It was necessary for them to be prepared for any eventuality. The great industrialists were alarmed at the prospect of the socialization of industry with its accompaniment of a partial or complete expropriation of their factories. They were prepared to make any concession in order to retain their property. They were ready to recognize Trade Unions, to accept an eight-hour day, and to agree to increased wages and the social demands of the workpeople. They were prepared to work in common with the Labour organizations and to settle all industrial questions jointly with the Trade Union leaders if only they could escape expropriation by these means. In the former Empire the Right Wing of the National Liberal Party had been the political mouthpiece of the great industrialists. In common with the Conservative Parties this section of the National Liberals was numbered among the victims of November 9. Both Conservatives and Right Wing National Liberals were compelled to reconcile themselves to the complete loss of political power.

* * *

The Soviets [i.e., councils] that came into existence in 1918 in Germany were true Soviets, and not the shadow creations that the Bolshevists permitted to exist in Russia. For no single Party in the German Revolution was capable of exercising a despotic dictatorship over the Soviets. The Majority Socialists, as well as the Independents, proclaimed their belief in self-government by the working class. The Spartacists were both too few and too weak to tyrannize over the German Workmen's and Soldiers' Councils. Moreover, the Spartacist leaders, especially Rosa Luxemburg, had sharply rejected the notion of any such Party Dictatorship over the proletariat.

On November 10, 1918, the Workmen's and Soldier's Councils wielded the actual power throughout Germany, both in the town and in the country, supported by the revolutionary groups in the army and by the working men who in many places also furnished themselves with arms. The great political question was whether the Councils would continue to rule in Germany, or whether they would be rendered useless by some fresh turn of events. In the Germany of 1918, there was really a dual government. For the former State and local authorities had not been abolished by the Revolution. The State and provincial governments carried on their work under the supervision of the Councils.

Hitherto Germany had not known the meaning of a living democracy, a real self-government of the masses. The State controlled public life; nor did so-called local autonomy afford a counterbalance. The great plan devised by Baron von Stein for setting up a middle-class State in Prussia had been curtailed and altered after Stein's retirement. Not merely were the local authorities restricted in all they did by the government of the State, but, worst of all, the important posts in the local administrations were occupied by long-term officials. The men who filled honorary and unpaid posts in the German Communal administration up to 1918 played a very small part in comparison with the professional Civil Servants.

Thus the masses of the German people were totally lacking in practical experience of managing their own affairs in a responsible manner. Bureaucratic control of public affairs rested upon a tradition of centuries. It appeared hardly conceivable that it should be vanquished by a revolutionary storm. True democracy, however, does not consist in registering votes on any particular question, but in the active self-government of the masses. The abolition of the bureaucracy was thus a question of life and death for German democracy.

The unique example of Russia and historical evolution now suddenly provided the German masses with the machinery of democratic self-government. The Councils were elected from the workers themselves, and were in the closest connexion with their electors, who might at any time dismiss them. They received no fixed pay but only essential allowances for expenses. Their task was to control all public activities in the towns and to intervene wherever necessary. During the Revolution only Soldiers' and Workmen's Councils had at first been formed. Outside Bavaria the Peasants' Councils were practically negligible. If government by the Councils were to persist, the fact that the Soldiers' Councils would in a short time be no more must be taken into account. For the army that had fought in the World War, and that numbered millions, must within a few weeks be demobilized. Instead of Soldiers' Councils there would have to be Councils formed by members of the trades and professions. Above all, Peasants' Councils would have to be organized throughout Germany. What particular professions were or were not admitted to the organization was a question of minor importance. If all those persons engaged in labour and in productive work were admitted to Councils, then at least 90 per cent of all adults had the right to vote. The question as to whether persons who were not engaged in productive work should be debarred from the right to vote was quite unimportant, because it affected only a very small percentage of the population.

It would have been quite easy to organize the Councils in the various parts of the country into Provincial Congresses, and from these to form a Reich Congress of Councils. The importance of the conception of government by the Councils does not lie in the particular form it should take

— whether the right to vote should be curtailed in this or that manner, and whether polling should take place in the factory or in the district where the voters reside. Its importance as well as its distinctive feature consists in the overcoming of the historic antithesis between executive and legislative by the substitution of self-government by a mature people for bureaucratic government of the people. In itself, government by Councils signifies neither a terror nor the tyranny of a minority, nor any fantastic experiments in the domain of economics. It would even have been possible — and this proposal was frequently made during the German Revolution — to combine the Councils in some way with the parliamentary system. A Consiliar Parliament, based upon the principle of the organization of the producers among the population according to their trades, might have taken its place beside popular representation of the old type. There were plenty of ways in which it was possible to conceive of the spheres of competence of the two parliaments being brought into relation to one another.

The Councils would not only have been faced with the task of assuring a true democracy to the masses of the German people. They might also have introduced important reforms in the economic sphere. After November 9, when the magnitude of the political victory of Social Democracy was clear to the masses, a cry for socialization was raised throughout the country. It is curious to note that the enthusiasm for Socialism was not the cause but a result of the November Revolution. In considerable strata of the population, not only among workers, but also among intellectuals, etc., there was a feeling that the old capitalist order had lasted too long and that it must give place to a new form of economic life. It is true that there was considerable difference of opinion as to what was to be understood by socialization. On one point, however, every one was agreed: that any form of planned or communal economy could only be successful if it mobilized the productive masses for active co-operation. And the organizations by which planned or communal economy was to be put into force were the Councils. The communal organization of a branch of industry could most conveniently be assured by the co-operation of the Councils of the individual factories or businesses. If socialization were to be more than merely bureaucratic State management, it could not dispense with the Councils.

What was the attitude of the individual Socialist Parties and groups to the question of government by Councils? The leaders of the Majority Socialists and the greater number of Party officials entertained little hope of the Councils. The historic ideal of German Social Democracy had been a parliamentary republic. The monarchical system had collapsed, and a German National Assembly was about to be elected on the widest possible suffrage. Moreover, the organs of self-government in all provinces and districts were to undergo democratic reform. This agreed with the long-standing demands of the Party and seemed better than any new-fangled experiments. The Majority Socialist officials regarded government by Councils as the arbitrary dictatorship of a minority over the majority of the nation. For they thought that the Councils were supported only by the workers in heavy industry, and would exclude the remaining masses of the population.

It is undoubtedly true that at that time large groups of the German people, even of the working classes, did not come within the sphere of the Councils. It is also true that in certain of the Workmen's and Soldiers' Councils local adventurers appeared and set themselves up as little dictators. These, however, were drawbacks that might easily be overcome and which were not an inevitable accompaniment of the Council system.

The Majority Socialist officials also rejected the idea of a Bolshevist tyranny and did not realize that Councils and Bolshevism were in no sense identical. Finally, the Majority Socialist Trade Unionists felt slighted and disturbed by the activity of the Councils among the workers. The German Trade Unions had for decades worked for the proletariat, and they now saw themselves being ousted by newcomers supported by the favour of the workers. The painstaking work of the Trade Unions could not be permitted to be endangered by the perilous desire of the Workmen's Councils for experiment.

The hostile attitude of the Social Democratic Party towards the Councils found its public embodiment in Ebert and Scheidemann. Nevertheless it would be wrong to attribute this mistake or many others of the revolutionary period to these two men personally. Many hundreds, indeed thousands, of respected Party officials throughout Germany agreed with Ebert and Scheidemann. These men quite rightly recognized the faults and shortcomings displayed by certain Workmen's and Soldiers' Councils. At the same time the conservative spirit of the Party was so strong in them that they were incapable of taking an unbiased attitude to new phenomena in political and social life. Thus Majority Socialism as a Party supported, as a matter of course, parliamentary democracy and the National Assembly. The Councils were looked upon merely as a transitory symptom. They were a product of revolutionary disorder, and they must disappear again as quickly as possible once the National Assembly and other parliamentary-democratic bodies had come into being in Germany.

These Majority Socialist officials were genuinely desirous of suppressing private capitalism and of strengthening Socialism at its expense. In the hopeless economic conditions which prevailed in Germany at that time, however, they were unwilling to make any economic experiments. They were anxious to avoid anything that might still further interfere with essential production. They wanted gradually and cautiously to transfer to public ownership only such industries as were, in the popular phrase, ripe for it.

The policy of the SPD in the question

of the Councils did not by any means receive the support of the entire Party membership. There were, in particular, thousands of Majority Socialists on the Workmen's Councils who were not prepared to take as narrow a view of their duties as the Party leaders prescribed. Nevertheless they were all in favour of the election of a National Assembly. But they wished the Councils to retain their competence beside the traditional Parliament. They expected the Councils to assist in safeguarding political democracy and in promoting nationalization.

* * *

The Council of the Representatives of the People shrank from the idea of any intervention in economic life. They did not wish to forestall the coming National Assembly in this matter. The Government summoned a number of experts to form a Nationalization Commission, and instructed it to discover which branches of industry were "ripe." On the other hand, the Council of the Representatives of the People could not make up its mind to pass laws interfering seriously with the conditions of private ownership. Nevertheless, intervention in the question of land tenure and also of mines was essential in the interests of democracy. The outworn system of large estates which dated from feudal days was at that time abolished in most European countries, not only in Soviet Russia, but also in the Baltic States, in Czechoslovakia, and in Roumania. An agrarian reform on these lines could undoubtedly have been introduced into Prussia east of the Elbe. It was not essentially a Socialist measure. Nevertheless the expropriation of the estates of the Prussian nobility and the parcellation of the land among the peasants would have made democracy secure east of the Elbe, and have put a final end to the power of the feudal aristocracy. The failure to nationalize the large estates and the disappearance of the Workmen's and Soldiers' Councils east of the Elbe brought a return

to the social and economic conditions of pre-War days there. Since the democratic republic had not the power to strike a blow at the Prussian feudal aristocracy it was unable to win the peasants over to its side.

Great differences of opinion existed on the question as to which industries were ready for nationalization. Nearly all Socialist thinkers, however, and also the great mass of the workers, were convinced that mining was one of them. To extract coal from the existing pits required no special gifts. It was a purely technical problem which was as easy to solve in a nationalized mine as in a privately owned one. Nationalization of the mines would certainly not have diminished production. But it would have made a great difference in the balance of political power. A particularly influential group of great industrialists, who had made their dominant influence felt most forcibly in the past, would thereby have been eliminated. The German republic would have remained a middle-class State even if the mines had been nationalized. Nevertheless the workers would have seen in such a step evidence of a serious desire on the part of the Government to introduce Socialism. Confidence in the new State and the new order would have been immensely strengthened among the proletariat.

The material objections made by the leading Majority Socialists to the nationalization of the mines were quite unsound. . . . It was further asserted that, while the Entente would respect private property in Germany, all public property would be regarded as pledges for reparations. Hence there was a risk that nationalized mines might be confiscated by the Allies. Subsequent events proved this danger to be non-existent. The German railways did not come under Entente supervision until 1924, as a result of the Dawes Plan; and the adoption of the Dawes Plan was a voluntary step on the part of Germany. The treatment of nationalized mines would have been no different from that meted out to national railways. Moreover, the Government might have found suitable means to compensate the expropriated landowners and mine-owners. It would have made no difference to the net political result.

The Representatives of the People did not touch the property either of the east Elbian landowners or of the coal magnates in the Ruhr district. A positive economic policy in the direction of Socialism would nevertheless have been possible even on the basis of the sanctity of private property. German industry might have been grouped in large syndicates. An economic programme might have been drawn up for each branch of industry, and the workers' Councils might have been given an important share in its execution. Even if such an organization had taken a long time to set up, the foundations at least might have been laid during the first few weeks. Such planned economy would have shown the Government's willingness to fall in with the desire of the working class for socialization, and the interest of the miners in production might have been stimulated afresh. Nothing of the kind was done. The decree of the Representatives of the People of December 23, regarding the wage agreements, did order committees of the workers to be set up in all industries and trades. These committees, however, were to concern themselves only with the application of the wage agreements, and with the personal affairs of the workers in the several industries and trades. They gained no influence over production. Since the Socialist Government of the Representatives of the People had no economic policy whatever, and simply allowed things to take their course, conditions became increasingly chaotic week by week in German industry. Angry and hopeless, the workers tried to extricate themselves from their difficulties by strikes, which only increased the general confusion.

Socialization Was Impossible

HERMANN MÜLLER

In replying to Third Way criticism, Social Democratic writers have argued that the critical economic and political conditions of the time precluded major social reforms, at least without the use of dictatorial Bolshevik methods. The fateful compromises were unavoidable—there simply was no Third Way. Hermann Müller defends this view in his memoir-history of the Revolution written in 1931. Even more actively than Rosenberg, Müller participated in the events he describes. As a leading Majority Socialist, he played a prominent role in the Executive Council appointed by the soldiers and workers of Berlin on November 10 to oversee the work of their newly created six-man provisional government called the Council of People's Commissars. He attended the First National Congress of Councils (December 16–21) and was chosen to serve on the new Central Council, created by the Congress to replace the Executive Council. In January he was elected to the National Assembly and later went on to become the parliamentary leader of his party, serving once as foreign minister (he signed the Treaty of Versailles) and twice as Reich chancellor in Social Democratic coalition governments.

WHOEVER OBSERVES the work of the People's Commissars objectively must admit that from the beginning they were not lacking in initiative. Two economic questions of special significance drew their attention: agricultural resettlement and socialization.

Gustav Bauer, state secretary of the Reich Labor Office, reported to the People's Commissars as early as the cabinet session of November 15 on suggestions for land resettlement. He had been in consultation with professors Sering and Oppenheimer. He received from the cabinet full authority to make the initial preparations. Occasionally the reproach has been made that the lands of the large estate owners were not divided up "by right of revolution," but these critics forget how difficult food conditions were then. Whoever possessed the least insight had grave fears for the winter and spring and saw salvation only in a coming good harvest. There threatened a repetition of the "turnip winter" of 1916–

1917. According to reports of Barth at a meeting on November 21, we would have after two months no more fat, after three months no more flour, and after five months no more potatoes. If developments in Poland cut off supplies from that area, the situation would become still more difficult.

Conditions soon became worse because the Spartacists in the Ruhr area, who had influence over a minority of the miners, obstructed the output of coal and thereby delayed the production of artificial fertilizer. In that desperate economic situation, not even a radical would have dared to change agrarian conditions drastically by revolutionary decrees. The consequence would have been the strongest opposition from the agrarian owners. The task was rather to lay hold of all foodstuffs with as little friction as possible and to distribute them.

The black market flourished. In the joint [SPD] meeting of the party council, the fraction of the National Assembly, and the control commission on March 22, 1919, I

From Hermann Müller, *Die November-Revolution: Erinnerungen* (Berlin: Verlag Der Bücherkreis, 1931), pp. 195–211.

explained in retrospect the political situation and the position of the party:

The black market is flourishing more than ever. Public morals have gone to the devil. What has become of our police-fearing nation? Herr Hugenberg perhaps does not have the right to make the warning: The German people had better become honest again. But in this matter he has hit the nail on the head. The few who have obeyed the law up to now no longer want to be the only stupid ones.

The question of socialization was then more in the air than the question of agricultural resettlement. The German Republic was proclaimed in the Circus Busch on November 10 as a "socialist Republic." The masses believed that it would be a simple thing to socialize the key industries by revolutionary decrees. Spartacus naturally made this a daily demand. But also *Freiheit,* the organ of the Independents [USPD], nourished at the beginning of its existence a belief in the miraculous power of the People's Commissars and the workers' and soldiers' councils. *Freiheit* demanded on November 16 that the government forthwith seize the large industries, which were so vitally important just at that moment, and declare them immediately to be national property: the mines, heavy iron, and related industries, likewise textile works, and the chemical, electric, and larger leather industries: "Our greatest enemy is fear of our own courage. . . . The government must decree an immediate confiscation of all important concerns. The financial settlement can come later."

For proof that all would go well they cited Ludendorff, who had made the industries in the occupied territories of France and Belgium work under forced military administration. *Freiheit* did not stand alone in this conception. Thus the Kiel workers' and soldiers' council, which was elected on a parity basis, unanimously adopted a resolution on November 22 which said: "Large-scale enterprises of industry as well as of landed property are immediately to be declared national property."

The Council of People's Commissars had said on November 12 in its proclamation to the German people: "The government called forth by the Revolution, whose political leadership is purely socialist, sets itself the task of realizing the socialist program."

The same proclamation, however, also said: "The government will maintain an ordered production, will protect property from interference by private persons, and will also protect personal freedom and safety."

Thus nothing definite was said about socialization. Barth maintains, to be sure, that he wanted to see accepted an additional passage about the anticipated socialization. It was resolved five to one, however, to leave the question of socialization open, as far as this proclamation was concerned.

On November 18 the cabinet decided to socialize those branches of industry which, in terms of their development, were ripe for it. At first a preparatory commission was to be set up.

Well-known socialists were called to serve on this commission: Heinrich Cunow, Rudolf Hilferding, Otto Hué, the leader of the miners, and Karl Kautsky; also the Berlin University professor, Karl Ballod, who in 1898 had edited for the Dietz publishing house under the pseudonym "Atlantikus" a brochure about the future state, *Production and Consumption in the Socialist People's State,* and whom no one in the old Empire knew to be a socialist. Moreover the professors E. Franke, the well-known Berlin social reformer, E. Lederer from Heidelberg, Robert Wilbrandt from Tübingen, and Dr. Theodor Vogelstein from Berlin were also called to the commission. Later they were joined by Paul Umbreit, editor of the *Correspondenzblatt* published by the general commission of the Free Trade Unions of Germany, and professors Schumpeter and Graz.

Walter Rathenau was originally also slated for the socialization commission. But the distrust which his name evoked in the ranks of the Independents eventually precluded his participation. . . .

The socialization commission convened on December 5, 1918 for its first session in the Reich Economic Council. In the meanwhile it had become obvious that the program of socialization would be a factor of enormous consequence for the whole recovery of economic life. Could the jump from a controlled war economy to socialization be ventured at all during this time of great uncertainty? Characteristically, a man whose strong field was neither theoretical nor practical economics was able to see further than the others: Kurt Eisner. He had revealed this already in the proclamation of the government of the Bavarian Republic on November 15, 1918, which said:

We consider it necessary to leave no doubt as to our unchanged socialist goals. But we declare with complete openness that it seems impossible to us, at a time when the productive power of the country is almost exhausted, to transfer industry immediately to public ownership. One cannot socialize when there is hardly anything left to be socialized. It is the conception of Karl Marx that the economy must be transferred to public ownership when the productive capacity has developed itself so extensively that it breaks through the too narrow shell of the capitalistic order. . . .

In the meantime the government of the People's Commissars realized that nothing had been done to implement the November 18 declaration of principle in favor of socialization. The state secretaries of the Reich Economics, Treasury, and Demobilization Offices had presented their deliberations to the People's Commissars. The latter had the enormous task of carrying out the transition from a war economy to a peace economy. One must consider that the export trade, which in peacetime had fed millions of workers and salaried employees, was completely cut off from most parts of the world. Where war industry had at first continued to operate, it was now demanded that it do so without profit.

The industrialists, who had to convert to peace, and who wanted to do so in their own interest, hesitated in placing contracts because the discussions about socialization made them fear that their plants might be seized. They were not at all certain in those days whether or not Germany would follow the sad path of Russia. This uncertainty made it difficult to absorb demobilized soldiers into normal economic life; indeed, actual lay-offs of workers were to be feared. Especially the older workers and salaried employees were fearful of losing their positions. The People's Commissars wanted to help as much as they could. State contracts were to be let. Further construction on the Mittelland Canal was immediately encouraged. The Reich, states, and communities were collectively to put up 1½ billion marks for housing construction. But assistance given by letting state contracts took place ultimately at the expense of the currency. The mark, as state secretary of the Treasury Schiffer reported on December 12, was already at 40 pfennigs. In addition, it occasionally happened in Berlin, in especially radical sections of the city, that workers simply tried themselves to take over businesses in the Russian fashion. The Executive Council had to concern itself with this kind of forcible socialization. In one case on See Street in Berlin, a 21-year-old chairman of a workers' council "socialized" the business in which he was employed, turning out the owner and confiscating the material. He based his actions on the authorization of the Executive Council. It turned out that Richard Müller, that human stamp machine, had let this document be stamped along with dozens of others that day, without anyone having noticed what it actually concerned. The Majority Socialist Büschel from the Executive Council had to intervene in the case. In the subsequent negotiations wage differences were settled but the owner was reinstated. The workers' council was to be "informed" about company proceedings as far as possible.

After several such incidents, deputations from big industry appeared before the People's Commissars and explained that they would have to shut down their plants if no security against such attacks could be given to them. The employers were not thereby resisting all state intervention in economic activity, since they wanted material support from Reich sources to create job opportunities and to satisfy their workers. The Employment Office, the Reich Economics Office, and the Demobilization Office recommended that state funds be given to stimulate economic recovery. State secretary Schiffer from the Reich Treasury Office, and his assistant Eduard Bernstein, had the strongest misgivings about such assistance. From an economic viewpoint they saw great danger in this subvention of the economy.

The creation of job opportunities, while retaining the capitalist system, in no way satisfied the workers. Intuitively they demanded socialization as the fruit of the Revolution.

Among the Independents it was especially Karl Kautsky who took pains to enlighten the working class about the extent of the collapse which was obstructing the fulfillment of their desire. He wrote in *Freiheit*:

To declare everything nationalized and then only afterwards set about to create the conditions requisite for nationalization means to put the cart before the horse, means to create a transition stage in which capitalist production is no longer possible and socialist production is not yet possible, a stage in which rational production is not possible at all. It means at least temporarily bringing production to a halt. To carry out — or even demand — such a socialization just now, at the moment of demobilization, would mean to turn Germany into a lunatic asylum.

For this Kautsky was denounced as a renegade by the Russian and German Soviet press.

That socialism meant construction and that construction was impossible without work, even the simplest workers realized. When the appeal for overtime was issued to workers in essential industries, it did not go unheard, despite the attempts of the

Spartacists again and again to sow discord. When the Independent *Freiheit* designated the achievement of the eight-hour day as a victory of the Revolution, *Rote Fahne* explained that naturally the eight-hour day was an obsolete bourgeois reform and demanded the six-hour day. If *Freiheit* had interceded for the six-hour day, *Rote Fahne* would have proclaimed the four-hour day as the next goal.

The Communists tried to ensnare the workers with the slogan: "Shorter hours and higher pay." That was certainly popular. But whoever had a sense of reality in those days had to beware of this slogan. The left radical People's Commissar Barth performed a great service when on November 25 in the Germania Auditorium he admonished the Berlin workers' councils to have greater understanding for the difficulties under which the People's Commissars had to work.

The time is not suited for experiments. Our plans must be carried out boldly, systematically, uniformly, and organically, in the interest of the general public. Socialization can take place only according to a uniform plan. He warned the workers not to conceive of the Revolution merely as a large-scale wage movement. If it were only that, it would soon be at an end.[1]

Those were worthwhile words, spoken at a meeting which was not devoid of fanatics. One of the delegates had recommended shooting a general and dispossessing a capitalist. Such examples would help intimidate the others. Naturally only people who had committed a crime were to be shot, as he added appeasingly.

The left radicals had no understanding of Barth's utterances. They did not recognize their Barth from the metal workers' strike any longer. In the second meeting of the Greater Berlin Workers' Council on November 29, Barth had to defend himself against the accusation made in Neukölln that he was a renegade.

[1] In this and several subsequent quotations, Müller appears to be using contemporary newspaper reports of public speeches. [Editor's note.]

He remained what he was, but he could not close his eyes to the facts. The German people could not produce raw materials from up their sleeves, and "one can only socialize when something is there to socialize." Today striking is no great art and requires no courage. One has to expect from the workers that they bring people to reason.

In the same meeting Kaliski called to the deified workers' councils:

"Don't confuse mass consciousness with megalomania." One could not play around with economic matters. The fate of millions is at stake. Political stupidities could be repaired, but millions would have to suffer for economic stupidities. Kaliski asked the workers' councils if they were prepared to take over the economic and technical leadership of the great concerns and answered to isolated calls of "yes" that he was glad only a few young elements had the courage for this "yes."

After a few ranters had cried out against Ebert and Scheidemann and their social patriotic brain trusters, I took the floor to reemphasize Barth's views:

I have just come from the provinces where the mass feeling against Berlin was fantastic. This ill humor was strengthened by the great many turbulent scenes in the meetings of the Berlin soldiers' and workers' councils and nourished by their unfruitful work. Our economic life can only get going, the unemployed can only find work, if a certain security is created which would permit advance planning. If we do not achieve uniform guiding principles and the authority to carry them through, we will soon sail into complete anarchy. If the workers' councils do not face up to the facts, we will soon have a social republic in form only, with no content. When I defended the People's Commissars, who had been installed as the provisional government by workers' and soldiers' councils, I was contradicted: "No, only by soldiers." I repeated: "If the government does not suit you, then turn it out." But you will be mistaken if you believe that only a handful of men stand behind Ebert and Scheidemann. The quarrel within the socialist ranks critically endangers the Republic. If the quarrel among the workers does not

cease, the socialist revolution will last only a few months, or even weeks.

My final appeal to bury the strife within the socialist ranks produced lengthy applause. That was proof of the fact that the majority of the workers' councils wanted assured work and sufficient bread in addition to the freedom already achieved, but were ready to abstain from impossible experiments. Only the leader of the revolutionary shop stewards, Wegmann, said at the same meeting of the Berlin workers' councils:

As long as the political immaturity of the great masses stands out so clearly, it is not possible to call a National Assembly. In the countryside the district councilors and parsons still have great influence. Thus the mood is not yet ripe for a National Assembly.

With similar utterances about the immaturity of the masses the Conservatives before the Revolution had defended the necessity of the three-class system of voting. Too much reaction and too much revolution lead to similar conclusions. With Wegmann's mistakes, the Majority Social Democrats were able to work very successfully among the workers against the left radicals. . . .

The leader of the German Iron and Steel Industrialists' Club, Dr. J. Reichart, gave a lecture on December 30, 1918 before the joint chambers of commerce of the Rhineland-Westphalia industrial district, in which among other things he explained:

Actually the situation was already clear in the early days of October. The question was: How can industry be saved? How can the entrepreneurs be preserved from the socialization threatening to engulf all branches of the economy, from nationalization and the approaching revolution?

On October 9, 1918 there sat in the Stahlhof at Düsseldorf a number of iron producers who conversed about these things. The assembled industrialists were in agreement that under existing conditions the government of Prince Max of Baden and Herr von Payer was untenable and that it would soon be over-thrown. The life span of this government was estimated at not more than four to five weeks (which unfortunately was exact to the day). In any event the iron producers could not hope for much from a weak government. If one looked further and asked, can the middle classes perhaps in the future become a strong support and help for German economic policy, one had to answer, in the face of many regretta-ble indications and frequent disappointments over the decades: Unfortunately, in economic policy matters, one cannot rely on the German middle classes in their present condition. Only the organized proletariat seemed to have a powerful influence. From that the conclusion was drawn: in the midst of the general uncer-tainty, in the face of the wavering power of the state and the government, industry can find strong allies only on the side of the work-ing class, that is, the trade unions.

Thus from their own most vital interests the industrialists made an alliance with the trade unions. But at a price. They had to surrender the principle which the fire-brands of heavy industry had defended most ardently, that of being "master in one's own house," the legacy of Stumm and Kirdorff. Moreover, the Working Agree-ment [of November 15, 1918] was the victory of a principle for which the trade unions had long fought, especially against heavy industry. The yellow [company] unions were excluded from the Working Agreement at the request of the Free Trade Unions. The eight-hour day, the May Day demand of the working class since the Paris Congress of 1889, was to be carried out without loss of earnings. By entering the Working Agreement and granting these concessions, the employers, to be sure, were only anticipating the demands of the People's Commissars.

The trade unions were not popular with the revolutionary council leaders. They had tried to achieve their popularity by fighting against the "union bosses." But even they realized that they could not get along without trade unions.

The Berlin trade-union commission de-clared that nothing could be undertaken in the factories without consent of the compe-tent trade-union organization and that the workers' councils, being political bodies, were not to interfere in the economic affairs of the factories. The Executive Council had expressly designated the trade unions as the bargaining agents in differ-ences between employers and workers. Employers sometimes took that as a pretext to turn away workers' councils when the latter presented grievances on behalf of the employees. In such a case the Executive Council was supposed to help the workers' councils. And it did, in the following regulation:

The various announcements of the Reich government and other governmental agencies, as well as the declaration of the Berlin trade-union commission are aimed at settling mis-understandings about the rights of workers' councils, workers' committees, etc. The em-ployers consider the workers' committees as already dissolved and refuse to concede to them any control over the concerns. With respect to this question, the Executive Council of the workers' and soldiers' council declares the following:
Pending the election of factory workers' councils, which will take place under the super-vision of the trade unions, the existing work-ers' committees remain in power. The control and co-determination of all questions arising from the production process belong to these workers' committees.

This resolution, as Richard Müller ad-mits in his book, *Vom Kaiserreich zur Republik,* was composed at a late hour in the Executive Council meeting without anyone understanding its import. By the later addition of detailed instructions it was virtually annulled before it had become effective. According to the new instruc-tions the factory councils had to settle all questions concerning the employees in concert with the factory management. On this occasion a halt was also called to the attempts at wildcat socialization, insofar as the Executive Council declared: "The socialization of concerns can only be under-taken by the socialist government, systematically and organically, in consideration of the whole domestic and external situation."

This did not suit Richard Müller. He demanded the control of the entire business operation by the workers' councils. If the employers dared to resist it, their resistance had to be broken. If necessary, one might proceed to the expropriation of obstructive employers! . . . .

At the First Congress of Councils Rudolf Hilferding spoke on socialization. Like the People's Commissars, he was for the transfer to social ownership of those industries that were ripe for it.

Ripe were coal mining, iron ore mining, iron manufacture at all levels, and potash mining. The nationalization of large estates was also necessary, especially forests.

Hilferding was himself a member of the socialization commission and was aware of the difficulties of carrying out these demands:

A political revolution is relatively easy to carry out. The execution of socialization means the substitution of one economic system for another. This cannot be done simply by a decree, but is a long and tedious process. Socialization means the realization of the highest social ideal, which can only be achieved by the collaboration of all social forces.

The Congress, after long debate, accepted a compromise resolution which instructed the government immediately to begin with the socialization of mining and the other industries ripe for socialization.

Hilferding in his report had rightly pointed out that the execution of socialization would require a socialist majority in the National Assembly. But since the elections for the National Assembly were so long delayed as a result of the agitation of the left radicals, and because the bitter battle between socialists and Communists repelled many workers and salaried employees, the National Assembly did not receive a socialist majority. And therewith emerged the strongest obstacle to the continuation of socialization efforts.

The question of socialization was also a subject of debate between the People's Commissars and the Central Council before the Independents withdrew from the government. Although the report of the socialization commission was not yet in hand, Ebert was ready for cooperation. He made the suggestion that the commission be summoned first of all to work out a plan for the socialization of the mines.

The socialization commission presented a preliminary report on its activity to the Central Council on January 7, 1919. It set up general principles for the socialization program along with its own plan of action. Its report asserted among other things:

It [the commission] proceeded on the assumption that nothing would be more dangerous than to transform economic life arbitrarily according to a general formula, that it depended much more on the levels of development and technical peculiarities of the individual branches of the economy whether and in what form they would each be accessible to socialization. Implicit already is the further principle that socialization is in no way understood as a blanket nationalization, but also includes, according to individual circumstances, the property of communities and other self-governing bodies, of consumer cooperatives, and finally various forms of public control and participation.

Decisive for all these questions, not only because of general socialist principles but especially in the present situation, is the concern to preserve and, if possible, expand the productivity of the economy. This concern also requires firm establishment of the principle that where property is socialized the previous owners are to be compensated, so that a disturbance or even breakdown of production can be avoided in the present critical situation.

Understandable as the impatience of the public to see a concrete realization of the socialist program is the commission would not do justice to its heavy responsibility if it worked out proposals without a thorough scrutiny of all individual questions, which in every case must be of the most decisive consequence to the whole life of the German people. Insight into the gravity of its task forbids the commission to give in to popular demand; the commission has from the beginning taken the viewpoint that only a thorough, methodical working out of individual problems can lead to the goal. . . .

The foremost means of state influence on industry during the war had been the requisitioning and allocation of raw materials. The shortage of raw materials, the lack of coal and workers, frequently had led to forced shutdowns and mergers of related concerns. This had taken place inorganically, however, according to the needs of the moment, while now a rational cooperation was supposed to take place. Since the employers were pressing for a quick and complete repeal of the entire control system, the socialization commission recommended that the People's Commissars alter or eliminate the control organization in individual cases only after agreement with the commission. It thereby sought to guarantee the government an influence on the rational reorganization of the economy during the transition to peacetime conditions. . . .

The socialization commission also deliberated thoroughly on the question of bituminous coal mining. The profitability of a government-owned operation was discussed. Before its work was finished, the socialization commission delivered to the People's Commissars the following declaration of principle:

The mineral resources of the German Reich are the property of the nation. The government is determined to make good this property right by taking back for the Reich the mining rights granted to private individuals, as far as they concern unexhausted fields, and by declaring in principle the transfer to the Reich of the property of all operating concerns. The question of managerial organization and the form of compensation remain for more detailed regulation.

In all cases the entire marketing organization, price determination, and decisions about the building of new shafts and the opening of new mines must be subject to state regulation and supervision. The mining rules of private individuals will be nullified at once. The relevant legislation will be worked out with the greatest speed.

The principles of shop democracy should be carried out legally. The elected representatives of the workers and salaried employees will be given an especially far-reaching influence in the determination of wages, hours, and safety measures. For this purpose they must be assured the necessary inspection of business management. This will also give them an opportunity to see to it that the technical encouragement of employees is taken into consideration. The guiding view for the entire concern will no longer be the capitalistic profit motive, but rather bettering the condition of the workers and salaried employees, and the total interest of society.

Thus far had the socialization commission proceeded by the beginning of January 1919, when the Communist rebellion shook the Republic so grievously that the continued existence of the provisional government was in question, and when 12 days still separated us from the National Assembly election whose results would decisively affect the fate of all efforts at socialization.

The National Assembly received a bourgeois majority. The Social Democratic Party did not on that ground give up the battle for socialization. Its necessity was emphasized in the March 1, 1919 manifesto of the party executive and National Assembly fraction. In the National Assembly the Social Democratic fraction introduced the following resolution on March 1:

The National Assembly wants to resolve:

1. The property of all mineral resources necessary for preservation of the economy belongs solely to the nation.

2. The Reich government is instructed to bring mines and energy production under public control (socialization) as quickly as possible, and thereby to give the workers and salaried employees, through suitable representation (work councils), a part in control and administration.

The Reich government promised to have worked out as soon as possible a draft law expressing these wishes. On March 3, 1919 after prior deliberation in the states committee of the National Assembly, there emerged a socialization law and a law on the regulation of the coal industry. The first was a skeleton law which gave to the Reich general authority to socialize industries, while the second transferred the future control of the German coal industry to a Reich coal council, in which employers, employees, and consumers had to consult with each other under the supervision of the state. Following the law regulating the coal industry was a similar one on the potash industry, for which the Reich potash council was created. These draft laws drew lively resistance from the bourgeois parties during the intensive discussions in the committees.

The decisive second paragraph of the socialization law reads:

The Reich is empowered through legislation and with adequate compensation
1. To socialize suitable economic undertakings, especially those engaged in extracting mineral resources and exploiting the forces of nature, and in case of pressing need to regulate the production and distribution of goods for the common weal.

A proposal to remove the words, "with adequate compensation" failed, because of the opposition of all the bourgeois parties.

Thus the possibility for socialization was there, but nevertheless socialization did not progress. The socialization of the "coal syndicate" was not the kind of socialization the workers had demanded. Unrestrained private enterprise was certainly restricted by the supervisory powers of the Reich. But this was still a far cry from socialism. After the dissolution of the National Assembly, the bourgeois majority hostile to socialization became even stronger in the first Reichstag. At the same time the extra-parliamentary strength of the proletariat became weaker.

After the defeat of the Spartacists in the Berlin January uprising, the Communists tried again and again to call out general strikes in the Ruhr area, in the Halle soft coal region and in Upper and Lower Silesia, with the slogan, "Socialization of key industries." If the Communists were politically defeated, they wanted to try by economic means to disrupt the new German Republic. The movements which this Communist slogan called forth not only hurt the workers who participated in them, but because of the resultant coal shortage condemned to unemployment the workers who did not participate. These strikes lacked any clear aim or central direction. A fire was started alternately, today in this district, tomorrow in that. Nothing was achieved in this manner, not even where, as in the Ruhr area in the early part of January 1919, a transitory united front of Social Democrats, Independents, and Spartacists was formed "to take the immediate socialization of the coal mines" into their own hands. Even that lasted only for a short time. Each united front with the left radicals carried within itself the germ of its own destruction.

The Socialists Not to Blame

KLAUS EPSTEIN

The debate over the Third Way has remained a lively one from the time of Rosenberg and Müller down to the present day. As mentioned in the Introduction, American writers have tended to sympathize with the Third Way and have criticized the Social Democrats accordingly. German-born historian Klaus Epstein takes three of them to task for this attitude in the following selection from a review article. Reaffirming that no third way existed, Epstein suggests that traditional American optimism has prevented them from grasping the essential tragedy of the Weimar Republic. He reviews the development of German socialism and finds that the moderate reformist policies pursued by the MSPD offered whatever small hope existed for the successful democratization of Germany in 1918–1919. Epstein was educated at Harvard and has written the principal biography of the Center Party leader, Matthias Erzberger, as well as a lengthy study of the genesis of German conservatism. He was professor of history at Brown University until his untimely death in 1967.

AMERICAN HISTORIANS dealing with modern Germany have been preoccupied with the problem of why that country failed to achieve an effectively functioning democratic structure which could resist the onslaught of Nazism. Gordon Craig, in *The Politics of the Prussian Army*, has sought the explanation in the uncontrolled power and anti-democratic outlook of the *Junker*-dominated General Staff. Leonard Krieger's *The German Idea of Freedom* analyzes the divorce in German liberalism between the ideals of liberty and self-government, which led to its emasculating compromise with the Bismarckian state. Klemens von Klemperer's *Germany's New Conservatism* chronicles the Conservative hostility to the democratic Republic which greatly, however unintentionally, benefited Nazism. The conduct of the Catholic Zentrum Party — so alien to American political traditions — has aroused comparatively little interest, but it is generally condemned for its authoritarianism and opportunism, culminating in its support of the Enabling Law in 1933. Thus the General Staff, liberalism, conservatism, and political Catholicism are all criticized for their anti-democratic outlook and conduct, and to American scholars the best chance for the achievement of German democracy seems to have lain in the Social Democratic Party (SPD).

The intentions of the German Socialists are generally lauded, while their practical failure is deplored. American historians have approached their record with a keen sense of disappointment. They do not expect anything good from such incorrigible sinners as *Junkers*, General Staff officers, or parties dominated by landlords (the Conservatives), heavy industry (the National Liberals), or priests (the Zentrum); but they do expect effective action from men whose outlook was dominated by democratic and socialist convictions. The Socialists' failure to democratize and socialize the Weimar Republic is explained by three distinguished scholarly studies dealing with the SPD in the period before and during the First World War. Peter Gay's *The Dilemma of Democratic Socialism* ex-

From Klaus Epstein, "Three American Studies of German Socialism," *World Politics*, XI (1959), 629–36, 642–45, 647–51. Reprinted by permission of *World Politics*.

amines Bernstein and the Revisionist movement. Carl Schorske's *German Social Democracy, 1905–1917* traces the wartime
schism back into the prewar decade. A.
Joseph Berlau's *The German Social Democratic Party* analyzes the wartime conduct
of the SPD. . . .

I

Gay emphasizes that the development of
a mass party headed by a bureaucracy and
appealing to many non-Socialist voters inevitably dampened revolutionism. So did
the remarkable prosperity which began in
1895 and disproved Marx's prediction concerning the increasing misery of the proletariat under capitalism. The rise of a
powerful trade union movement, whose
leaders were *de facto* Revisionists, however
indifferent to problems of theory, made a
moderate reformist course for the SPD inevitable. Gay states convincingly that if
Bernstein had not existed, it would have
been necessary to invent him. Bernstein
was not responsible for the party's evolution from revolutionism to reformism: he
only gave intellectual respectability to this
transformation. Revisionism was no more
than the theoretical sector of the larger reformist movement, not its cause: it cannot,
therefore, be held responsible for all the
results of reformism. . . .

Bernstein's political theory called for the
achievement of democratic ends by democratic means. He believed in the general
spread of parliamentary democracy, and
thought this would make the application of
violence — abhorrent in any case — unnecessary. He expected socialism to advance
within the capitalist framework through
trade union activity, co-operatives, and social legislation. His prescription for achieving socialism in Germany was co-operation
among a Revisionist SPD, a democratic left
bourgeoisie, trade unions, and co-operatives,
with the purpose of securing a *Reichstag*
majority. Such a coalition would legislate
social reforms, nationalize industries when-
ever a clear economic advantage could be

demonstrated, promote equality by restrict-
ing the disposal of private property, and
generally use the existing state machinery
to achieve socialist ends. Bernstein ridi-
culed the Marxist dogma of the withering-
away of the state, and deplored the very
thought of a minority proletarian dictatorship. Gay no doubt rightly accuses Bernstein of underestimating the intransigence
of German right-wing forces, who would
not easily abdicate their position to a mere
parliamentary majority. But he also shows
that Bernstein did not rely exclusively upon
parliamentary methods. Bernstein ignored
trade union shudders in his advocacy of
the idea of a general strike under certain
circumstances, such as the upper classes
seeking to eliminate the existing democratic
franchise by a *coup d'état*. This was a
logical position for Bernstein to assume:
precisely because his political program depended upon the exercise of the democratic
franchise, he must support all steps — including non-parliamentary violence — required for its survival.

Gay's attitude toward these Revisionist
views is curiously mixed. He admires Bernstein's fearless pursuit of truth, and admits
that he was right in many of his substantive
views, especially in the field of economics.
Yet he finds that Bernstein left many logical
problems unresolved, and obviously believes that Rosa Luxemburg — the most
brilliant and extreme anti-Revisionist —
had a far superior brain. He finds Bernstein fundamentally an honest but rather
muddled thinker who lacked thorough
philosophical training. This patronizing
judgment would be justified if Bernstein
had attempted to set himself up as a great
systematic theorist. But the whole point of
his revisionism was that logic and dogma
had led Marxism into a cul-de-sac: what
was needed to guide the movement was
empirical common sense untroubled by possible logical difficulties. Bernstein provided
just this, and he should not be judged by
criteria which were irrelevant to his purpose.

Gay's second major criticism is that revisionism, while admirable in a country like England with deep-rooted democratic-parliamentary traditions, was inapplicable in a Germany dominated by intransigent right-wing forces. He believes that Bernstein was deluding himself in his view that the powerful *Junker*-industrial classes could be dislodged from power by mere parliamentary pressure: he therefore believes — though he indicates this more by implication than by direct statement — that the Luxemburg radicals were right and the Bernstein reformists wrong. Gay is clear in his general statement of what constitutes the "dilemma of democratic socialism" in a non-democratic country: to achieve socialism by democratic means is impossible in the face of intransigent reaction; yet to seek power by non-democratic means — i.e., revolutionary violence — is to risk — if successful — the establishment of a totalitarian socialism. Although he never argues the case explicitly, Gay believes that the second course, despite its dangers, was preferable in the specific situation of Germany. He ignores the fact that revolutionary violence could not possibly have been successful in Germany, and that if temporarily successful — say, through the exploitation of a military disaster like that of 1918 — it would have provoked a bloody civil war which the socialist radicals could not possibly win. He ignores the strength of Germany's anti-socialist forces, conservative, liberal, and Catholic — and the probable reaction of the other European powers. The radical wing of the SPD never faced up to this fact, and neither does Gay. It is perfectly true that the prospects facing a Revisionist SPD policy were, admittedly, also gloomy, but what small hope existed of establishing socialism in the foreseeable future depended upon the triumph of revisionism. Only an alliance with the left wings of German liberalism and Catholicism offered any real chance of strengthening political democracy in Germany, the indispensable prerequisite for social democracy; any such alliance presupposed a prior victory for revisionism within the SPD. A *de facto* revisionism

was inevitable in any case in the light of the political, economic, and institutional factors mentioned above. Only a parallel acceptance of Revisionist theory could have ended the absurd prewar situation of an SPD which acted in a Revisionist manner while continuing to use a radical, bloodthirsty, atheistic, and republican jargon. The dualism between actions and words was dictated by a concern for party unity, a theme which is discussed brilliantly in the Schorske book analyzed below. Suffice it to say here that this dualism prevented the SPD from reaping the advantages of either moderation (possible alliance with other forces) or radicalism (preparing a revolutionary nucleus for future contingencies). . . .

The Revisionist program failed in Germany, but it must be emphasized that it was never given a fair trial by the party. Its champions were thwarted by the Radicals before, the Independents during, and the Communists after the war. Yet if German social democracy is ever to gain power, it must surely build itself squarely upon the liberal, humane, and anti-doctrinaire attitude of Bernstein.

* * *

II

Schorske's condemnation of the party bureaucracy contains a quixotic element. Bureaucratization is an inevitable development in any large modern organization, and reliance upon spontaneity is a prescription for impotence, as Schorske notes himself in his discussion of the USP. His moral indignation is directed against the reformists who used their party position of power to censor revolutionary views. Yet the radicals, on the occasions when they controlled the party, wished to expel the Revisionists in 1903 and the Baden budget supporters in 1910. The use of institutional power to influence ideological controversies is inevitable in any party. It should rather be emphasized that the SPD executive usually tolerated remarkable divergence of opinion in the party. There was freedom of discussion at the annual congress, and an anti-executive candidate lost election to the executive in 1913 by the narrow margin of 269 to 211 (p. 280). The party leaders strove heroically to maintain party unity by constant verbal concessions to the radicals at a time when the radical policy of active revolutionism was sheer nonsense. It is true that party unity was purchased at the unfortunate price of dualism between rabid talk and sheepish action. But even unity on such unsatisfactory terms was preferable to the complete impotence which a formal split would have brought to radicals and reformists alike. No doubt the party lost its capacity for future revolutionary action through its bureaucratization, succumbing to trade union influence, making a fetish of unity, and becoming preoccupied with electoral victories. But every one of these tendencies was inevitable under the tranquil and remarkably libertarian conditions of Wilhelmine Germany. A really revolutionary party like that of the Bolsheviks could develop only under Tsarist conditions, which happily did not exist in Germany. The SPD executive took the sensible view that revolution in Germany was unthinkable in peacetime and undesirable in wartime. The sole chance of successful revolution lay in the exploitation of a military defeat such as actually occurred in 1918. Schorske's criticism of the party's loss of its revolutionary potential implies that the SPD should have geared its outlook primarily to the contingency of an Imperial collapse through war. But is it not asking too much to require it to have abandoned successful electioneering, the trade union alliance, and a consequent reformist mentality, in order to become a pure revolutionary party prepared for one contingency only? Moreover, democratic socialism — the proper goal of the SPD — could scarcely be established in Germany by revolutionary means, since the latter — even in the improbable case of temporary success — would necessarily have tended toward totalitarian tyranny.

Schorske does not sufficiently emphasize the intrinsically tragic position of the SPD in German society, with the extreme unlikelihood of the establishment of socialism even if the party executive had consisted of angels instead of bureaucrats. A policy of radical revolutionism could only have provoked merciless police repression; a reformist alliance with other parliamentary forces was most unlikely to overthrow the *Junker*-capitalist ascendancy. The existence of competing radical and reformist wings within the party was inevitable under the circumstances. The two alternatives confronting the SPD were equally undesirable: to opt for either an exclusively reformist or a radical policy meant a party split; to refuse to make a choice meant a muddled, illogical centrist line which would kill revolutionary *élan* while yielding no practical results, and at the same time would frighten potential liberal allies by doctrinaire theory while disgusting the radicals by tepid passivity.

The poor prospects for the SPD were thus rooted in the German realities which produced these unfortunate alternatives, not in specific faults of the leadership. Bebel, who despite failing health retained a firm grip upon party affairs almost until his death in 1913, was certainly an impressive leader. It is one of the few faults of Schorske's book that he never explains Bebel's double role as both the brake and the spur of the party, or explores his personality, with its curious mixture of enthusiasm and idealism, caution and opportunist prudence. Bebel sought to avoid both the adventurism of the radicals and the loss of fighting *élan* of the reformists, and it was circumstances rather than choice which made him more successful in the former than the latter. He at any rate never became completely identified with either faction, and he succeeded in his primary aim of keeping the party together. Bebel had participated as a young man in the conflict between the Lassalleans and Marxists, which in some ways anticipated the post-1905 conflict between the reformists and the radicals (though Schorske finds, after careful examination, that there was little continuity as postulated by Berlau). He had learned the value of unity at that time, even if it was purchased with some compromise and much confusion. The main weakness of his position was the absence of any clear-cut view on how the SPD was to seize power. He was less troubled by this than he ought to have been, because he accepted the Marxist formula — denied only by Bernstein's Revisionists — that the capitalist world was inevitably moving toward socialism. Let the party stay together until the moment when general social forces made Germany ready for socialism — then socialism must come, and no one could accurately foresee whether revolutionary or reformist means would be appropriate at the appointed moment. It was foolish to rule out either possibility completely. But the SPD must, in the meantime, use the opportunities of constitutional agitation and trade union advance which Imperial Germany offered. This involved, no doubt, the danger of opportunism and excessive bureaucratization, problems which Bebel certainly recognized: he may have preferred Haase, the man of the left center, to Ebert as co-chairman in 1911 for this very reason. It is probable that he made greater concessions to the radicals than any other leader would have made. The radicals were frustrated by a conspiracy of circumstances rather than of men.

III

Joseph Berlau's *The German Social Democratic Party, 1914–1921* reads in some ways like a partisan USP tract. . . . The book concentrates on the war, the revolution, and the peace settlement. Berlau's main thesis is that the SPD betrayed its principles and succumbed to opportunist tactics in meeting each of these crises. He deplores that the revolutionary, class-conscious, and internationalist party of the Erfurt program (1891) became the reformist, democratic, and nationalist party of

1919. Berlau feels that German democracy was the loser in this evolution from straitlaced Marxism to what he calls a policy of "compromise, opportunism, and circumspection" (p. 330). It meant that the so-called revolution of 1919 brought "no clear break with the economic, social and foreign aspirations of the German Empire and its bourgeois supporters" (p. 339). He notes that, while Germany changed little, the SPD changed much, and he seeks to explain the former regrettable phenomenon in terms of the latter. The book is presented as a case study of the results flowing from the SPD betrayal of its Marxist principles.

* * *

Berlau is very hostile to the policy of the SPD throughout the revolutionary winter of 1918–1919. Ebert's insistence that the party enter the Cabinet of Max von Baden is condemned as "Millerandism," and Berlau deplores the willingness of the SPD to co-operate with the Zentrum and Left Liberals as symptomatic of how far the party had moved to the right. He neglects to mention that the two coalition partners had, meanwhile, moved far to the left of their prewar position. Berlau condemns the SPD hostility to the November revolution, ignoring the fact that the so-called revolution was primarily a naval mutiny which came at the worst possible moment, while Germany was in the middle of delicate international negotiations. He ridicules the failure of the SPD to press openly for the abdication of the Emperor. He forgets (when he does not deplore) that participation in a coalition government always involves a degree of self-restraint, and that republicanism was not a sufficient reason for breaking up a government which was the sole alternative to chaos.

Berlau's most vitriolic attack is directed against the record of the SPD after it secured the major share of governmental authority in November 1918. "The ideals expressed at Erfurt and the expectations based upon the revolution could not have been disavowed more decisively than by the zeal of the successful revolutionaries to resist the enactment of their own traditional program" (p. 338). Berlau accuses the leaders of (1) failure to enact their socialist program by decree before the meeting of the Weimar Assembly, (2) specifically abandoning socialist goals both at that time and thereafter, and (3) succumbing to nationalism in their foreign policy. Furthermore, he feels that their abandonment of their own program not only hurt German democracy, but hurt the standing of the SPD with the electorate as well. Berlau argues that because the party aligned itself with the bourgeois parties, "it failed . . . to carry more conviction and influence than did the liberalism of those other parties which had been discredited by their impotence and lack of efficiency under the Empire" (p. 12).

These criticisms may be taken up in turn. It is true that Ebert refused to create a socialist *fait accompli* prior to the elections for the National Assembly. To have attempted to do so not only would have been anti-democratic in principle (whether or not that is to be viewed as an objection), but would have provoked civil war and required Bolshevik methods to achieve any measure of success. The bloodshed, chaos, and famine resulting from such a policy (whether successful or not) would have provided an even worse foundation for the creation of German democracy than that upon which Weimar was actually built.

The criticism that the SPD became lukewarm about certain socialist goals is far better taken and is, from a strictly socialist point of view, unrefutable. Many SPD leaders declared socialization to be impracticable even after the establishment of the new democratic government had minimized the danger of chaos and civil war. They emphasized that socialism could not be built in a country dependent upon international trade, because it allegedly increased the costs of production; least of all could it be built in a country where four years of war had demoralized any idealism

which might replace capitalist incentives. SPD theorists also saw the difficulties presented by each of the two possible forms of socialist organization. The first, ownership of the enterprise by the workers employed in it, would create only a new kind of selfish and inefficient workers' capitalism; the second, direct control by the state, brought all the rigidities involved in bureaucratic administration. The latter objection also applied to the concept of a planned economy developed in 1919 by Wissell, the Socialist Minister of Economics and his assistant Moellendorf, which secured remarkably little SPD support. The party distrusted Workers' Councils, the natural home of leftist troublemakers, though it reluctantly accepted them to buy off a series of strikes which afflicted Germany in 1919. All these views of the SPD leadership were perhaps sensible, and one could even congratulate the party for abandoning the demagogic follies of opposition when achieving responsible power; but Berlau is quite right that the party abandoned an essential part of its program without any absolutely compelling excuse, unless it be common sense. . . .

Berlau's belief that the moderation of the SPD proved a disadvantage at the polls is also dubious. It provides him with a *deus ex machina* through which Germany could have — despite circumstances of unparalleled difficulty — secured a democratic and socialist republic in 1919. He believes that an SPD minority program of socialization, decreed as a *fait accompli* before the elections of January 1919, would have converted sections of the inert but anti-socialist majority of the German people to socialism, prevented the secession of radical workers to the KPD, and given the party a majority in the subsequent elections. Berlau has contempt for the "unguided and hence static will of the public" (p. 260) and accuses the SPD of "devaluing the concept of democracy" (*ibid.*) and especially democratic leadership, by abstaining from strong socialist action out of deference to the presumed views of an anti-socialist majority.

His view that the SPD would have won the January 1919 elections on a more socialist program is certainly false: the party attracted millions of ordinarily non-Socialist voters at this time, precisely because of its moderation, its democratic views, and its firm stand against socialistic experiments and Spartacist insurrection. The tragic fact is that socialism could not be achieved in 1919 by democratic means, and that to seek it by Bolshevik means meant civil war which the Socialists could not win or could win only by turning Germany into a Communist despotism. . . .

It is characteristic of American scholarship that all three authors here examined sympathize with the left wing of the SPD, and believe that the failure of the party was primarily due to the excessive moderation of its leadership as it was molded by bureaucratization, trade union practice, and Revisionist theory. They all — though Schorske less than Gay and Berlau — level moral reproaches against the SPD leadership, and do less than justice to the enormously difficult situation which the German Socialists faced. American historians are handicapped when dealing with tragic German developments by the deep-rooted American faith that all problems can be solved by intelligence and good will. They refuse to accept the view that the problems confronting German Socialists were in fact insoluble, and that whatever line of conduct the leaders took — be it moderation or radicalism — they were most unlikely to achieve their objective. American historians have underestimated the impersonal forces and conditions which made German Socialists act as they did, and have engaged in an essentially futile search for villains.

The Ruhr Miners and the Third Way

PETER VON OERTZEN

The work of the young Göttingen historian, Peter von Oertzen, figures prominently in a recent German revival of Third Way scholarship. To rebut the conservative critics of Rosenberg (represented in this essay by Karl Dietrich Erdmann), von Oertzen gives close scrutiny to the Ruhr miners' movement of early 1919. In this and similar movements, he finds hope for an effective socialization under council control which—had it been accepted and encouraged by the Berlin government—might have provided the foundation for a more lasting democracy in Germany. Reference to the author's full-length treatment of this subject may be found in the bibliography at the end of the volume. Von Oertzen has also recently served as a Bundestag deputy of the Social Democratic Party.

ALL RESEARCH in the history of the Weimar Republic is dominated, as K. D. Erdmann rightly emphasizes, by the question of the causes for its collapse. With this question in mind certain topics present themselves as especially important. One of them, the revolutionary origin of the Republic, will be examined here. This topic is also the center of Arthur Rosenberg's book, with which — also according to Erdmann — begins the scientific investigation of the period of German history from 1918 to 1933. Rosenberg's thesis is that Social Democratic leadership during the Revolution failed to create firm foundations for a real democracy. The democratic movement which came into power in November 1918 would have had to destroy the social and political positions of the hitherto ruling anti-democratic powers in the army, in the state apparatus, and in the economy, and would have had to set up "a new popular democracy." The starting point for "a living democracy, a meaningful self-government of the masses," which Rosenberg sees in the council movement, should have been developed instead of suppressed by the Social Democratic leadership. Because of this failure the young republic was deformed from the hour of its birth.

The Rosenberg thesis is not lacking in appeal and historical investigation should come to grips with it more than has been the case up to now. Thus Erdmann emphasizes in opposition to Rosenberg that the Republic came into being as a socialist-conservative marriage of convenience, because of the failure of the social revolution. That is quite right but behind it lies the question: Is a democratic constitution viable at all if it rests, like the Weimar Republic, upon the misalliance of completely opposed social forces? And Erdmann circumvents this question.

There is scarcely a doubt about the important role the army, the bureaucracy, and industry played in the dissolution and collapse of the Republic. And it is obvious that the preconditions for this role were created to a considerable extent in the revolutionary period at the beginning of the Republic.

The incomplete social integration of the

From Peter von Oertzen, "Die grossen Streiks der Ruhrbergarbeiterschaft im Frühjahr 1919," *Vierteljahrshefte für Zeitgeschichte*, VI (1958), 231–33, 238–44, 246–58, 261–62. Reprinted by permission of *Vierteljahrshefte für Zeitgeschichte*.

socialist working class and its political division were also of great significance for the fate of the Weimar Republic. The democratic parliamentary system was blocked by the absolute hostility of the radical left; the collaboration of the Social Democrats, loyal in itself, was frustrated by continued class conflict; and in all crises of the Republic the internecine socialist struggle paralyzed the defense of democracy. Both the schism and the incomplete integration of the socialist working class were likewise rooted in the conditions created in 1918 and 1919.

To expose these roots at one point is the purpose of the following study. It will concern itself exclusively with a certain facet of the socialization question. Its result is limited and — seen in terms of the whole — provisional, for any attempt to settle the open questions in the history of the Revolution from a single reference point must necessarily fail. Beyond this is the fact that there are to this day no satisfactory investigations of such important problems as military policy in the Revolution or the attempts to undertake a democratic reform of the administration. Also in an initial stage is the investigation of the council movement and its meaning.

The question of socialization — next to the problem of armed force — had extraordinary significance and crucially influenced the attitude of the working class toward the democratic Republic. In what manner and how far it did so is worth investigating. In this connection arises the extremely delicate but unavoidable question, what would have happened, if . . . ? the question whether Social Democratic policy toward the workers' desire for socialization was objectively founded and necessary or whether it was not. If this question can be answered and the effects that the failure of socialization had on the proletariat can be measured, then discussion of the Rosenberg thesis will have taken a step forward.

A question such as the one formulated here is only meaningful if the revolutionary period can be conceived of as a genuine turning point in which alternative paths were really open. Whether this was the case must be tested. But one may not simply assume the current interpretation and declare apodictically that in 1918–1919 there was no real third possibility between a red army and a Reichswehr under the leadership of the old officer corps, between a proletarian dictatorship and a democracy built up in alliance with conservative forces. By asserting this, one blocks the way to Rosenberg's suggestion of an "interim period" in which these alternatives had not yet become binding. The obvious task is not to reject his suggestion from the outset, but to test it exactly, and if possible to deepen it, to complete or concretize it.

* * *

II

It is not possible within this small frame to present a complete picture of the entire social movement of the year 1919 in Germany. Indeed, it would lead too far even to select only the decisively important events in the entire movement. But among these there stands out above all others the great strikes in Western and Central Germany and in Berlin from January to April 1919. In connection with these the so-called "pure council movement" of the left USPD and the disputes over the creation of a work council law from spring till late summer, 1919, deserve greatest attention. All these phenomena are interconnected in various ways. Because of its structure and effect, however, the socialization movement of the Ruhr miners may lay claim to a special position in this matrix. It began the earliest, lasted the longest, and reflected most clearly the elemental forces within the movement that were not yet organized or ideologically formed. Our study can thus limit itself to this phenomenon without doing too much damage to the whole.

To begin with, the external development of the movement must be briefly described.

The political upheaval of November 1918 had generally taken place in the Ruhr district without serious disorder. But in the same month mutually independent movements began in different places that put forth material and social demands of the most varied kind. In the foreground were the desires for increased wages, shorter hours, compensation for the six shifts of wages withheld as punishment in the miners' strike of 1912, etc. Changes in working conditions were also demanded very emphatically: above all they demanded that the unorganized join the unions; then, new election of workers' committees, recognition of the unions, relaxation of management controls, abolition of the mine-inspector system, changes in punishment procedures, and almost everywhere the removal of unpopular superiors. The movements did not always remain within the conventional framework of an orderly strike. Not infrequently the demands were forced through by threats of violence. This was especially true in the mines of the district on the right bank of the Rhine. Above all Hamborn and Mülheim developed at that time into focal points of the syndicalist "Free Union of German Trade Unions" and were centers of radical activity. The regular unions disapproved of these spontaneous movements, were anxious about the sinking production of coal, and called for peace. The miners, however, were not satisfied with the agreement for an eight-hour day and a moderate raise in wages which the old federation of trade unions had already attained on November 15. The strikes and disturbances continued. In the week before Christmas there were for a time as many as 30,000 men on strike.

In the course of the general political developments, particularly after the break between the SPD and the USPD in December 1918 and in the wake of the Berlin January disturbances, conflicts in the Ruhr area became intensified and politicized and not infrequently led to bloody clashes. Strike movements in the mines increased. Unrest was multiplied on the one hand by the putschist undertakings of left radical groups (in Dortmund on January 7 and 8, in Gladbeck on January 11 and 13, in Düsseldorf on January 8 and 11, and in Duisburg on January 11 and 13), and on the other hand by the first engagements of security forces and the newly formed *Freikorps* (in Gladbeck on December 17, in Hagen on January 8 and 9, and in Buer on January 14).

At the turn of the new year demands for socialization first came to the fore. This development was certainly influenced by the First Congress of Councils. The revolutionary parliament, meeting in Berlin from December 16 to 21, 1918, had not only called for the prompt election of a National Assembly, thus committing itself to parliamentary democracy, but had also instructed the government "to begin immediately with the socialization of all mature industries, especially mining." Under the slogan of socialization and the concomitant council system the general mass movement acquired a more conscious, i.e., increasingly political, character. The wave of strikes reached a new peak. On January 11 more than 80,000 miners were on strike.

In the face of this serious and, in the long run, untenable situation, the Essen workers' and soldiers' council, in which all three socialist parties, SPD, USPD, and KPD were represented, seized the initiative. On January 9 it decided to proclaim by itself the socialization of the mines. On January 11 it occupied the offices of the coal syndicate and the mine owners' association in Essen, decreed a general wage and price control, and demanded from mine managers and workers a resumption of production. It appointed one of the lawyers belonging to the SPD, the magistrate Ruben, to be the people's commissar for preparing the socialization of the mines, and placed at his side deputies from the three socialist parties. A proclamation signed by all the parties asked the workers to end all strikes immediately. At the same time a conference of all the workers' and soldiers' councils of the Rhine-Westphalian industrial area was called in Essen for January 13. At this conference representatives of the Reich government and the trade unions took part. In agreement with them the conference unanimously decided for the immediate socialization of the mines. Ruben was confirmed as people's commissar, and by his side was placed a commission composed of three representatives each from the SPD, USPD, and KPD — the so-called "Commission of Nine." Moreover, the election of a council organization for the Ruhr area itself was called for. The workers were asked to resume work immediately. On the following day an election procedure was issued and the immediate holding of the council elections arranged.

The strikes, which had already slackened off gradually after January 11, stopped abruptly. With the exception of a limited wave of strikes between January 18 and 22, first and foremost in the always restless Hamborn, the district remained calm until the middle of February. A small number of local strikes formed an exception, but these were caused predominantly by the conduct of the employers. The latter refused — understandably from their viewpoint — to give their consent to the Essen resolution and tried in several cases to hinder the election of councils in the mines. They cited the December 23, 1918 decree of the People's Commissars, which envisaged the election of workers' committees with limited rights, and declared that they wanted to sanction only such workers' committees in their plants.

The Reich government likewise showed no inclination to sanction the Essen resolutions. It arranged for the election of work councils (of course on the model of the committees rejected by the workers) and appointed three commissioners of socialization — the union leader Hué, the general director Vögler, and the privy mine councilor Röhrig. Beyond that it promised the establishment of "work chambers" with limited rights. It was not, however, entirely prepared to acknowledge the newly elected councils and the activity of the Commission

of Nine. Indeed, only with hesitation did it decide for the above-mentioned measures.

In two further conferences on January 20 and February 6 the workers' and soldiers' council of the Ruhr area confirmed once again, almost unanimously despite increasing tension in their own ranks, the resolutions of January 13. They declared their complete readiness to cooperate with the government and the appointed socialization commissioners. To be sure, in the February conference the increasingly impatient delegates demanded a clear acknowledgment of their demands and threatened a general strike for February 15 in case of rejection. At the same time they appointed in place of Ruben, who had already been removed on January 22, the Communist Dr. Julius Marchlewski (Karski) as economic and journalistic advisor to the Commission of Nine. The government refused again to acknowledge the council system and the Commission of Nine, and began making preparations for a military intervention in the district.

On February 11 the newly appointed Commander of military district VII, General Watter, dissolved the soldiers' council in Münster, which was known to be especially radical, and had its members arrested in order to forestall a presumably imminent Spartacist uprising in all of Northern Germany. This action produced a great outcry among the workers, who were already viewing the military measures of the government with extreme distrust. The radicals insisted on the carrying out of the threatened general strike and on the disarmament of the *Freikorps*. A conference called in Essen on February 14 decided in favor of the general strike and for armed resistance to the *Freikorps* in case the government did not immediately undo the measures in Münster. On February 15 troops moved into the northern part of the district, in Hervest-Dorsten, because several days before a bourgeois politician had been murdered, and bloody battles ensued. Thereupon a partial conference of workers' councils called by the radical side decided to enter the general strike immediately. The ultra-radical syndicalists dominated this Mülheim conference, and their unscrupulous maneuver was of great consequence.

On February 18 the regular conference of the workers' and soldiers' councils convened in order to hear reports on the results of negotiations going on with the government. But they never got around to it. Right at the beginning of the session tumultuous disputes broke out between moderates and radicals about the Mülheim strike resolution. The overwhelming majority of the Social Democratic participants left the conference; those who remained proclaimed the general strike. Thereupon the Social Democratic representatives left the Commission of Nine and the four trade unions (Free, Christian, Polish, Hirsh-Duncker) declared themselves against the strike. The troops entered the industrial area, producing bloody encounters in some places with terrible outrages on both sides. The strike was not everywhere carried out, even though the strikers in some places did not shrink from terrorizing the non-strikers. At the peak on February 20 there were about 180,000 men on strike, hardly more than half of the miners. On February 21 the strike was officially broken off by a delegates' conference and collapsed in a few days. The end result was immeasurable bitterness on all sides, which led not only to continual clashes with the troops but also to bloody disputes within the working class itself.

* * *

III

Now that the external course of the miners' movement has been related, we must ask and try to answer . . . questions about its social and political character.

1. In the course of the events described, did a radicalization of the Ruhr area working class take place?

There is no doubt that after 1920 in almost all elections in the Ruhr area the left radical votes heavily outweighed the Social Democratic ones, that the district became a center of proletarian radicalism in the Weimar Republic. The question is whether the course of the movement in the spring of 1919 contributed to this result. One can hardly offer an incontestable answer. The problem of radicalism and radicalization in the working class is many sided and cannot be reduced to a simple formula. The thesis opposed to our own, that radicalization did not determine the fate of the miners' movement, but rather that an already deeply rooted radicalism among the miners caused the failure of their movement, may have sound arguments in its favor. We will have to return to them in more detail. But one important fact speaks against such a thesis from the outset. The movement quite obviously began as a relatively moderate one and only gradually became radical in the course of its development.

In February there was still strong resistance to the general strike slogan of the left and the warnings of the trade unions and the SPD found an audience. In many places the strikers tried to induce the non-strikers by more or less forcible means to stop work. Despite this pressure, scarcely half of the miners took part and the strike collapsed quickly. In April, under a state of martial law, strike terror was neither possible nor necessary. Participation was almost twice as large as in February and the endurance of the strikers unusual. (One must remember that the unions paid no strike funds, and that the strikers had thus to make heavy material sacrifices.) The SPD and the unions no longer had the slightest influence on the strikers; the unions saw themselves forced to make concessions far beyond their actual intentions, in order simply to save their organizations. These concessions did not prevent at least the free [i.e., socialist] miners' union from suffering heavy and permanent losses and from seeing the influence of the radical wing increased considerably within its own ranks.

An equally effective argument for our thesis lies in the fact that between the middle of January and the middle of February, thus at the time when the movement was still united and appeared to be successful, the district was calm, which it was not either before or after. That is all the more remarkable because at the same time all over the Reich the bloody pacification actions of the newly formed *Freikorps* were in progress. One may try to deny any connection between the general calm and the Essen socialization measures, but the fact of the calm itself is beyond all doubt. With a few local exceptions — usually springing, as we have seen, from the refusal of the employers to recognize the Commission of Nine and the newly elected councils — there were serious collisions only in the notoriously restless and radical cities of Hamborn and Mülheim. They occupy a special position because of the local dominance of the syndicalist "Free Union of German Trade Unions" which was just as bellicose as it was without discipline. But the disturbances there were only of a local nature and without fundamental political significance.

That the general calm was a direct result of the Essen action can scarcely be questioned seriously. Even the first call contained a passionate appeal to the workers to forego all striking from then on. And it did not stop with mere words. Delegates and members of the Commission of Nine influenced local movements in a moderate and orderly direction. Even the Communists did not exclude themselves from its effect. The People's Commissar Ruben, in his various utterances on the miners' movement, has likewise emphasized the profound effect of the socialization measures and has given himself the credit. An additional and especially convincing proof for our interpretation is provided by a report which the Social Democratic deputy and later president of the government of Arnsberg, König, gave on February 24, 1919 before the Central Council of the German Republic in Berlin. In his presentation, which is filled with extreme hostility toward the radical left, appears nonetheless the following final judgment on the main point at issue, the council question: "Instead of working the councils into the existing order of the mines, the government only permitted the system of mine councils to be proclaimed from case to case. It should have been carried out generally. Then we would have had peace." According to the opinion of this leading Social Democrat, a timely and honest recognition by the government of the council system decided upon in Essen could have prevented the outbreak of the general strike in February.

2. The answer to this first question leads directly to the second, whether a broad unified socialist middle current existed in the working class that transcended party lines.

Such a current did exist. The mere fact that at a time when the bloody so-called "Spartacus disturbances" were taking place all over Germany, Social Democrats, Independents, and Communists collaborated for four weeks on the basis of a common program, is conclusive enough. This unity was forced upon the leaders by the workers. Only thus can one explain how programmatic declarations at three conferences could be almost unanimously accepted and put into force by representatives of all tendencies, even though the party organization leaders, both right and left, were half-hearted in their support.

Not even the KPD ventured separate undertakings, despite the heavy influence precisely in the Ruhr area of ultra-radical elements that later split off into the Communist Workers' Party (KAPD). The official party account in 1929 violently criticizes the "illusions" of the movement and reports also that the Essen local of the KPD, "after lively disagreements," disapproved of cosigning the Essen manifesto of January 13. Indirectly it thereby confirms the almost complete unanimity of the Ruhr miners on their established platform. For the SPD and the unions also there was nothing to do but go along; even the

Christian trade-union leader, Center Party member, and present under-secretary of state, Gieberts, spoke words of approval at the Essen conferences of January 13 and 20. How irresistible the workers' pressure for united action must have been is revealed once again in König's report before the Central Council. "So as not to have the movement undertaken by the Spartacists alone, the Independents (sic!) and the Majority Socialists agreed to enter the commission. I have the impression that Hué (the union editor and actual leader of the free miners' union) let himself be dragged along and thus we got into this unpleasant situation," namely to have to stand for four weeks in a common front with Spartacists and Independents on the basis of a decidedly socialist program. In fact, this was for the party of Noske a more than peculiar situation.

After the disintegration of the movement, Social Democracy and the unions understandably tried to separate themselves as sharply as possible from the Commission of Nine and its activity. These attempts cannot eradicate the fact that Social Democratic representatives participated in the work of the Commission of Nine down to the last moment. The Social Democratic pit foreman Stein was chairman of the Commission of Nine and presided over the Essen conference of February 6, which threatened the government with a general strike, as well as over the negotiating commission appointed by the conference; and in these negotiations on February 13 and 14 he supported the Essen program unreservedly. Even in their official declarations of February 18 and 19 against the general strike, the Social Democrats still declared themselves for the Commission of Nine, for the institution of councils, and for socialization, while they disassociated themselves expressly from the state secretary of the Reich economic office, Dr. August Müller, who was cool toward socialization.

These impressions about the movement are confirmed by an investigation of its programmatic statements. The appeal, "To the Population of the Ruhr Coal District,"

signed by representatives of all the socialist parties and distributed after January 13, is an extremely remarkable document to which we will return. In this connection it is noteworthy that the demands set forth are very moderate in form and content, that attention is called several times to the collaboration of the unions, and that the appeal for the unity of the working class pervades the entire document.

3 and 4. The question of the danger of a council (soviet) dictatorship in the Russian sense — i.e., the danger of "Bolshevism" — and the question of the Spartacist secret control which was supposed to have been behind all the unrest can be answered conclusively and rather briefly.

The practice and program of the movement do not permit any other conclusion, as must be clear from what has already been said, than that the council system and socialization were intended as an extension of parliamentary democracy, not as its replacement by council dictatorship. The Commission of Nine strove to the last day of its activity to become legalized by the government and the National Assembly.

It cannot be overlooked, of course, that in January there were left radical putsches in several cities — most notably in Düsseldorf — which aimed more or less openly at a council dictatorship in the political sense; and one should not underestimate the frequent and occasionally quite violent undertakings on the right bank of the Rhine. But all these isolated attempts, in which little revolutionary vanguards made the most of general dissatisfaction, or only the general insecurity, stopped — with few exceptions — as long as a moderate policy satisfying the majority of the workers appeared to be successful. In other words, it is undeniable that there was a small, very active putschist minority. This is true of the whole revolutionary movement. But this minority remained without influence as long as the broad socialist movement in the working class kept its solidarity.

The report which Karski gave on March 5 on the problems of socialization provides a confirmation of these facts. Although bitterness was intense over the unsuccessful general strike, although the audience was predominantly radical, and although the speaker was a revolutionary Communist, the tenor of the address was exceptionally moderate. The Russian model was expressly set aside as not binding, and the concept of the dictatorship of the proletariat as a terrorist minority dictatorship was rejected. The next stage of the movement, to judge by Karski's address, is a stage of socialist government which carefully but resolutely begins the socialization program and otherwise secures the control of key economic positions for the workers. There is no question of inciting rebellion; the first step, on the contrary, is the agitational and organizational strengthening of the socialization movement. It need not be asked whether Karski's actual plans possibly went further, it is only important that even in this circle and in this tense situation he did not consider it wise to demand more.

The question of alleged Spartacist control of the movement can be dismissed with a few words. All the documents and incidents discussed here testify convincingly to the spontaneous nature of the movement. Who could have formed a revolutionary headquarters? The USPD had disintegrated into several hostile tendencies; and its organizational development was far from complete in the spring of 1919. Perhaps the supporters of a pure council system in the left wing of the USPD (Däumig, Richard Müller, Stoecker, Brass, Koenen) could have provided the leadership for a bold revolutionary policy. That they did not succeed in providing such leadership, and on the basis of their organizational and political weakness could not have done so, is shown incontestably, and with open self-criticism in Richard Müller's memoirs. The syndicalists, who were especially influential in the centers of radicalism, rejected all central organization and political discipline on principle. It would be complete nonsense to suppose that they would have let themselves be directed by an external secret control. The newly established KPD was organizationally hardly more than a

sect and besides — particularly in the West — was anything but unified. Moreover, the Communist policies, insofar as they were influenced by the national party leaders in those months, certainly did not countenance immediate revolt.

The putative Communist plan for a general uprising in January 1919, advanced in several quarters, is a legend. Reference to the January battles in Berlin proves the opposite: it is an incontestable conclusion of historical research that the so-called January uprising was anything but a planned action. It was much more an entirely unprepared and spontaneous response to a special situation; moreover, the assertion that paid provocateurs had a hand in the game finds several arguments in its favor. The supportive putsches in Bremen, Düsseldorf, and a few other cities — undertaken while Berlin was in revolt — represented spontaneous thrusts by local party leaders who took the Berlin rebellion more seriously than it actually was.

A further consideration to be advanced against allegations of the Spartacist control of the whole movement is the fact that in the Ruhr area — as in the Reich at large — the leading radical proletarian party, politically and organizationally, was not the KPD but the USPD. And this party, as we have seen, was neither willing nor able to pursue a policy or revolution at any price. Besides it was not the relatively pro-Communist left wing of the USPD that dominated in the important Westphalian section of the Ruhr area, but a moderate faction that had an absolute aversion to all putschist adventures.

5. A very important question, and one not easy to answer, concerns the underlying impetus of the movement. From beginning to end, without any doubt, the miners' demands for improvement of wages and working conditions stood at the center of their desires. The demand for pay raises and above all shorter working hours played a decisive role throughout. If "socialization" had appeared only as a general rather than a concrete goal, one would be justified in considering it merely a slogan brought

into the movement from outside for agitational purposes. But contrary to such an assumption, socialization appears in the thinking of the movement as an absolutely concrete undertaking. It presents itself as a political, social, and economic process in whose course the mines are appropriated by the general population and the workers, and whose first stage is the setting up of a council system and the control of production by the workers. This first step in the process of socialization originated obviously from a direct need of the miners, but it included more than the wish for an improvement in their material living conditions.

Nowhere in prewar Germany did the employers persist so stubbornly in their "master in one's own house" viewpoint as in West German heavy industry; in no other branch of industry, moreover — partly for traditional, partly for practical reasons — was the internal hierarchy of the concerns so rigid as in mining. The desire to strip employers and managers of their almost unlimited authority and to limit work regulations to what was technically necessary grew directly out of these conditions. The councils were supposed to help meet this desire by serving as organs of co-determination and control within the firms. Along with the urge for co-determination, in view of the general economic crisis and the employers' stubborn rejection of almost all of the workers' material demands, there developed a desire to gain access to the business policies of the firms. The organs of the Central Council were to undertake this task, especially the Commission of Nine. In this sense also the Essen workers' and soldiers' council justified its action on January 11, thereby expressing a doubtless widespread desire.

Beyond that, at least the socialist inclined miners (and this circle then extended far beyond the number of formal Social Democratic supporters) were of the opinion that such a profound attack on the traditional industrial structure would not be possible or lasting without a change in the general political and social conditions, especially not without the exclusion of the former

masters of the mines. These changes were for them the very content of the idea of socialization. Socialization and the council system consequently formed an inseparable unity in their minds.

Out of this desire to gain a voice in the management of the mines grew a readiness, on the basis of the newly acquired insight and responsibility, to limit their own demands. At least the leading figures in the movement were ready to subordinate wage demands to broader social and political responsibilities. In his previously mentioned address, Karski defined the new position of the miners, in sharp contrast to private and state capitalism, as "trustees" of society, who should administer the mines jointly with government economic leaders for the common interest. And this idea corresponded exactly to the views of the Commission of Nine.

The movement has been reproached from all sides with the charge that the miners — in the sense of a primitive syndicalism — wanted only to seize the mines, run them alone, and distribute the proceeds among themselves. Such ideas were, to be sure, not completely absent among the simplest supporters. But precisely the leaders of the movement did not allow themselves so to be swayed. And this fact cannot be obscured by all the accusations, obviously produced by strong emotions, that were directed above all against the "Bolshevik" Karski.

6. With that we come to the last and, in a certain sense, most important question, which concerns the creative and constructive elements of the movement.

Such elements were obviously present in the behavior of the workers. This emerges unambiguously from the documents of the movement. Of special importance are the January 13 appeal, "To the Population of the Ruhr Coal District," and the Commission's brochure on socialization. The appeal expresses the sense of the movement in a few simple words: "The people's commissar and his associates should not . . . rule from above like the old authorities, but should be carried forward by the confidence of the entire working class. Therefore it has been decided to build the work of socialization on the council system." All unions and parties are in agreement on this question. What is needed now is self-discipline, a feeling of responsibility, and dedicated work. Strikes from now on are "an antiquated remedy," for "the council system is better than striking."

The authors of the Commission's brochure formulated the same ideas more sharply and with a polemical turn against the Social Democratic leaders by whom they felt themselves betrayed. These leaders imagined socialization to be an act "which should be proclaimed from above . . . in the bureaucratic-parliamentary way. The active participation of the workers in this task seems a horror and an abomination to these freshly hatched excellencies." Not that the workers want to overthrow everything, "for the pitmen are not so ignorant that one could not make clear to them that socialization is an undertaking which cannot be carried out from one day to the next." But the workers demand tangible guarantees that are given them by the council system through which the employers are to be carefully controlled in the mines, in the employers' associations, in the coal syndicate, and in the coal office.

The concrete proposals for the construction of the council system are absolutely sensible. The above-mentioned appeal does not claim exaggerated rights for the councils that are to secure the "co-determination of the working class." They should "oversee" and "regulate" things "together with the management." The stipulations about the competence of the pit-foreman district councils and mine councils are similar, and were worked out with the active collaboration of Social Democratic trade unionists in the weeks following the first Essen conference. The district councils receive a completely equal right of co-determination in questions of working conditions and wage-setting. The mine councils are empowered to so determine the order of work, the imposition of punishments, the dismissal of workers, and the mediation of disputes between district councils, workers,

and officials. Besides this they could receive on request "the right to inspect all the operational, economic, and business records of the firm." Finally, the central councils are to oversee the large employers' associations and to prepare for socialization.

Special value was attached to the collaboration of technical and commercial officials. The first appeal of the newly formed Commission of Nine addressed itself to this problem. The "united front of hand and brain workers" also lay at the center of the conflict in the election of the councils, for the old workers' committees excluded officials from employee representation. The employers tried by every means — even withholding salaries — to prevent officials from finding solidarity with the workers. The workers on the other hand took great pains to get expert advice. The appeal of Ruben and Karski similarly reveals a manifest readiness to cooperate with the government socialization commissioners. The resolution of the January 20 Essen conference, which tries to create a workable "central body for socialization" with subcommittees and expert advisory councils, points in the same direction.

In the face of the evidence presented, it is difficult to understand how so serious and benevolent an observer as Emil Lederer, scarcely one year after the event, could write that these "wildcat socializations" were a matter of "rebellious disturbances," without plan and without the capability of arousing a spirit-lifting political movement. It seems that Lederer, looking from afar and not as a direct participant, has confused cause and effect. The movement failed to attain a positive configuration because it lacked governmental support and could not develop; it did not remain isolated because it contained no fruitful possibilities.

Moreover Lederer's severe judgment does not even completely apply to the "wildcat socializations" actually carried out in at least a partly revolutionary way. In a number of mines the workers had forced the removal of one or more of the higher officials. By no means, however, did that always happen in an entirely indiscriminate way. In several cases the decision, if obviously in error, was later corrected. This happened for example at the Werne mine, about which the workers' and soldiers' council very objectively reported to the Central Council of the German Republic, differentiating itself sharply from "Spartacist intrigues." At the Viktoria-Lünen mine an obviously capable pit foreman, Schürken, with the help of some of the officials, independently demanded the removal of the mine management, and apparently not without success.

All these facts were unfortunately obscured by contemporary and later political polemics. If, for example, the trade unions later raised the heaviest reproaches against the work of the Commission of Nine, these should scarcely be accepted without question. The moderate forces, as we saw, cooperated actively until the middle of February and had equal rights. Similar reservations are also appropriate for attacks on individual leaders of the movement.

That the workers were generally ready and able to learn and to correct themselves can be seen, for example, in the new election of the Commission of Nine in April, when several publicly criticized representatives did not turn up again, while capable and experienced men, such as the above-mentioned pit foreman, Schürken, and the previously mentioned trade-union official, Teuber, were newly elected.

* * *

IV

A constructive socialization policy and a meaningful collaboration with the eco-

nomic council movement would have been completely possible in the spring of 1919. The endeavors of the SPD and USPD to unite just after the catastrophe of the January uprising were serious and honest. At least a renewed coalition of both parties and a firm unity of action could have come into being on the basis of a new policy, in which socialization would have formed an essential component. The formation of the *Freikorps* would then have become superfluous. The blood of the battles from February to May need not have been shed. The radical left would not have offered themselves as such cheap targets to their opposition; they would have remained weaker and would have had to be more moderate. To suppress the actions of a few hopelessly blinded utopians — as Rosenberg very correctly remarked — would have been merely a police job. That such a policy could have secured democracy better than what actually happened is an obvious conclusion.

The leaders of Social Democracy — and the main responsibility rests with them — did not take this path. It would be a separate undertaking to ascertain to what extent their decision was objectively founded in the overwhelming difficulties of the domestic and foreign situation, and to what extent in limited vision or personal failings. Without doubt Ebert and his friends tried honestly to serve democracy and simultaneously — true to their traditions — to promote the welfare of the working class. But the workers did not thank them for it; rather they turned away from them in great masses. And not least because of this, the main goal of Social Democratic policy in 1918–1919, the securing of democracy, was not achieved.

IV. THE TREATY OF VERSAILLES

Versailles Oppressed the Republic

GOLO MANN

Without its international context, the creation of the Weimar Republic cannot be understood, nor can its prospects for life be assessed. For Germans after June 1919, the basic fact of international relations was the Treaty of Versailles. Was this peace settlement shortsightedly harsh? Did it punish the wrong Germans, cripple the fragile new democracy, and revive a vindictive nationalism and militarism? Most friends of the Weimar Republic—German and non-German alike—have argued thus, often very bitterly. Without rancor, but with essentially the same viewpoint, the German historian Golo Mann explains the terms of the settlement and their effect on Germany. Mann's admirable ability to rise above the national passions of the time can no doubt partly be explained by his unique background. Son of the world-famous novelist Thomas Mann, he took his degree at Heidelberg in 1932, but spent many years in exile teaching in France, Switzerland, and the United States, before returning to Germany following World War II. In addition to his history of Germany, from which the selection below is taken, Mann has written the major biography of Metternich's advisor, Friedrich von Gentz.

HENCEFORTH Germany was to live under two basic laws. The Treaty of Versailles governed its relationship with its former enemies, with the outside world. The Weimar Constitution gave new form to its domestic conflicts and endeavours.

The peace treaty was a misfortune, only explained — there is no question of excusing it — by the fact that misfortune usually leads to new misfortune, that the men who had directed the war, and directed it in the way they had, could not now transform themselves into men of peace. Wilson, the American, wanted to break the chain of evil and to establish justice wherever there had been injustice. This he failed to do. Justice could only have been established if all states, nations and people concerned had been just. As long as they were not —

and there was no reason to suppose that they would be at this bleak, grim, vindictive moment of history — there could at best be practical solutions, careful compromises between power and power, between the wishes of the weak and the hard facts that had become history; there could be no "justice."

The American professor who wanted to cure the world with a panacea brewed up in the tidy laboratory of his mind fell out with his European partners — particularly with the most pessimistic among them, the French Prime Minister, Clemenceau. Wilson stood for naïve, young, powerful America for which the war had been fun. Clemenceau stood for exhausted, tragic France. The old man who could forget neither 1918 nor 1871 (when he was

From Golo Mann, *A History of Germany Since 1789* (London and New York, 1967), pp. 343–347. Translated by Marian Jackson. Reprinted by permission of Chatto & Windus, Ltd., and Frederick A. Praeger, Inc.

83

thirty), had only one thought: to preserve for France by means of hundreds of cunning tricks the position gained by such terrible sacrifices but untenable in the long run without the help of its allies.

The product of this clash of attitudes was repulsive: a close-knit mesh of regulations, intended to be "just" and unquestionably so in many details, but allowing injustice inspired by malice, hatred and the intoxication with victory to slip in wherever possible; so much so that the whole, in spite of individual examples of justice, seemed an enormous instrument for the suppression, exploitation and permanent humiliation of Germany. Whatever wrong Prussia-Germany had done in the 150 years was to be redressed: the Polish partition of 1772 — the new Polish state was given Posen and West Prussia, so that East Prussia was once more separated from the main body of Germany; the annexation of Schleswig-Holstein — there was to be a plebiscite in north Schleswig to enable those who so wished to join Denmark; naturally Alsace-Lorraine was to be given back to France and there were to be other, smaller, clumsier frontier rectifications. There were to be plebiscites in any place where there was a possible majority that might not want to remain in Germany, such as in Upper Silesia, in parts of East Prussia. Yet plebiscites were not allowed in countries that did not belong to Germany and the majority of whose inhabitants now probably wanted to join Germany, such as in Austria, in northern Bohemia. The new concept of legality — that a people must determine its own fate — was applied where it could harm Germany, not elsewhere; in the same manner as the Germans had applied it at Brest-Litovsk against the Russians. The Allies were happy to let the Brest-Litovsk settlements stand, in so far as any control of the chaos in the East was possible. They welcomed the fact that Germany had weakened Russia by the application of "just" principles and they were glad to weaken Germany by applying the same principles. The rest was a scuffle among the new or Successor

States which tried to expand as much as possible at the expense of Germany, Russia and each other, using historical, statistical, economic, national or linguistic arguments or just the right of the stronger. What became clear in the process was that "justice" was unobtainable even if there was no powerful unjust force to prevent its establishment. The three unjust giants, Russia, Germany and the Habsburgs had been defeated; yet the Poles and the Lithuanians, the Czechs and the Poles and the Slovaks, the Hungarians and the Rumanians, the Yugoslavs and the Italians were still incapable of ensuring that justice was done among themselves. Lloyd George said angrily to the Polish negotiator in Paris:

We, the French, the British, the Italians and the Americans, fought for the freedom of the small nations, which you had not the slightest hope of obtaining without us. You know that I myself belong to a small nation and it hurts me bitterly to see how all of you, before you have even crawled into the light of freedom, want to oppress nations or parts of nations that do not belong to you. You are more imperialistic than Britain and France.

By drawing political frontiers for Germany based on the result of doubtful plebiscites a dangerous precedent was established. Nobody, however, imagined that Germany could one day use this principle for its own ends; or asked what might become of central and eastern Europe then. For the moment Germany lost a tenth of its population — of which about half spoke German — an eighth of its territory, the major part of its iron ore and a substantial part of its coal — immense assets whose value was not calculated because their loss was intended only to redress old wrongs. The same applied to the colonies; they were taken from Germany not because it had been defeated but because it had by its barbaric behaviour proved unworthy of possessing colonies. On the same grounds the victors did not annex Germany's colonies outright but had their administration and exploitation transferred to them by the new League of Nations. These were self-righteous, greedy and short-sighted tricks; dissimulations that one does not like to remember and that would best be forgotten were it not for the fact that otherwise the rest of the story becomes incomprehensible. These deceptions hung like a millstone round the neck of the new German republic and oppressed the future of Europe as the great war itself, had it been terminated with a modicum of sense, could not have done. Mutilated Germany, further condemned to various immediate deliveries — locomotives, ships, cables — from its war-ruined stocks, was called upon to bear the blame for all the damage which the war — its war of aggression — had inflicted on the allied nations. No one knew the amount involved or over what period it was to be paid. Only this much was clear: the sums at stake could be increased arbitrarily, depending on what was included in the losses of states and civilian populations, and surpassed all imagination.

We have learnt something since then and such an iniquitous folly as "reparations" was not repeated at a later period which also had its follies. We know today that the wars of this century are bad for everybody and that the victor cannot undo the damage done to him by doubling or increasing a hundredfold that done to the defeated enemy. If he tries to do this he multiplies the damage done to himself. Victory is an illusion. The Paris peacemakers did not know this, and if we criticize them for it we should remember that influential Germans were equally ignorant and had intended to mete out to the Entente the treatment that Germany was experiencing. Let us not linger over examples of the blindness of statesmen and experts who here revealed themselves in all their human frailty. Let us only say that the principle of reparations as applied by the Treaty of Versailles created thirteen years of chaos and folly and that it could not do otherwise. Europe was much too densely populated, too small and too poor to be divided into two parts, one that paid and one that was

paid for. This did not mean that Germany should not have made an honest contribution towards rebuilding the ruined French and Belgian territories. It could and should have done so; and it was ready to do so.

An American journalist reporting the Paris negotiations wrote: "We are going to have a League of Nations, weak, wrong, capable of great abuse; and we shall get a peace also, full of dynamite which will burst into war." About the peace-makers he said:

The rulers of the world have sat here with the problem of human living before them, laid out on their table by the tragedy of war. That should have opened their minds and hearts to tackle the job in some new, big way. They wanted to. There was good-will here. But their old habits of mind, their fixed attention upon things they do not really want, their age, their education — these have made it impossible for them to do their work.

Not only the diplomats but also the nations were to blame for the bad treaty: "Only I see very clear here how it is not merely a class division, but an issue which divides every human heart against itself. Every little peasant and working man wants both his revenge upon the foe, his share of the recompense for injury done *and* no more wars." These were two conflicting wishes, the one cancelling out the other. In fact what the peacemakers in Paris had promised to do was neither new nor unprecedentedly just, but old and bad: "Consciously or not they are all working, fidgeting and intriguing to get back to the point where they stood before the war. . . . But the world cannot reverse gear; it cannot. It can fall or decline, like Greece or Rome, but it can never reverse gear." The journalist, Lincoln Steffens, an intelligent critic, was as disappointed by the attitude of the Germans as by the peace treaty; but more about that later.

It is an old truth that one should place least trust in one's own right, in one's own power and its duration when one is on top; then is the moment for humility, the moment to doubt of one's own merit. There is always something in victory to be ashamed of. The guilt of the peacemakers of 1919 lies in the moralistic superiority with which they treated the defeated enemy; having all sinned heavily themselves during the war, albeit with differences of degree; and being all about to sin heavily again. They had a right to impose this or that condition on the vanquished, but not to decree that he alone was responsible for the war, thereby anticipating historical research. Nor should they have founded a League of Nations in which they did not believe and for the realization of which they were not prepared to make sacrifices or great moral efforts; as a result they sullied and spoilt the whole idea for a long time to come. It is bad to reach for the sublime with an impure heart.

The German government signed the treaty. The paragraph on war guilt and reparations, the limitation of the German army and navy to the size of those of a small state, the occupation of the Rhineland for fifteen years or more, the separation from the Saar whose mines France would exploit — everything was accepted. But not approved. The Germans signed under protest because they had no choice. They called the treaty a "dictation" which indeed it was; because genuine negotiations had taken place only between the victors, not between victors and vanquished. Such a treaty does not last longer than the political situation on which it is based. The vanquished observes it only as long as he is defeated and weaker than the others. He has no moral obligation to observe it. And, given the world, and the way in which the balance of power is eventually redressed, it was unlikely that the Versailles treaty would last long. The only question was how it would be revised. This depended on both sides, on Germany and the Western powers.

Indignation in Germany was fanned by the belief of the Germans that they had been deceived; they had surrendered believing in Wilson's just peace programme, but the peace which they had been given, although bearing some relation to the Fourteen Points fell short of them in spirit, as a whole. What the Germans could not and did not wish to understand was simply that when Germany requested an armistice in October 1918 for moral and military reasons it no longer had any claim to Wilson's programme. It ought to have accepted the "just peace" while it could still do wrong or abstain from doing wrong; while it was still a power. After Ludendorff's sudden "we are lost" it was no longer a power and its appeals to Wilson's noble principles sounded hollow and morally false. The good-natured, stupid German Michael had surrendered voluntarily because he believed in the American gospel when he could have fought on and won — that was what the rabble-rousers now told the Germans. If it was untrue the truth was complicated and unpleasant. Why worry too much about it?

Those whose indignation was loudest were those who were most to blame; who for four years had contemptuously rejected a moderate peace; who had been determined to impose on the enemy conditions at least as brutal as the Treaty of Versailles, and who then suddenly and at the worst moment had cried "we are lost." They directed their false anger not so much against the outside world as against part of their own people. Against the left, politically speaking. Against the parliamentarians who for years had preached restraint and who had been called upon too late to assume responsibility; who had not wanted capitulation in October 1918, the men of the Social Democratic Party, of the Centre. They were now presented as the real criminals. Had they not assumed power or the semblance of power at the very moment of military catastrophe? Were they not spiritual brothers of the Entente, these democrats, these supporters of the parliamentary system and of the new American gospel which had proved such a terrible failure? Had they not signed the treaty in spite of the protest of the Conservatives, or as they now called themselves the *Deutschnationalen*? It was easy to forget that the Supreme Command had advised or ordered the treaty to be signed, particularly as Hindenburg had happened to be out of the room when the Chief of Staff, Groener, stated the army's views for the last time. Those who bore the greatest guilt pretended to be innocent. Those who were innocent or much less guilty appeared as the creators and as true, typical representatives of the Versailles system.

The peace treaty affected Germany in two ways. It created a distorted, unnatural relationship between Germany and the world, its neighbours to the West and the East; and it divided the nation because one group of politicians and their supporters quickly found themselves insidiously being made to shoulder the responsibility for every misfortune. They protested, but not very vigorously nor very successfully.

Allied Power Sustained the Republic

A. J. P. TAYLOR

Contrasting radically with Mann's opinions are those of the renowned Oxford historian A. J. P. Taylor. In the selection below, not only does Taylor defend the justice of the Versailles Treaty but he goes on to assert that, far from crippling German democracy, Allied power kept the Republic in existence from start to finish. The reader will note that the selection was written at the close of World War II when anti-German feeling was understandably strong. He should likewise be wary of Taylor's known weakness for provocative statements, for shocking and sometimes perverse interpretations. But he must also be aware of Taylor's extensive and highly respected scholarship, especially in the field of Central European affairs. His books in this field include a study of German colonialism, a biography of Bismarck, and a history of the Hapsburg monarchy.

THUS, IN February 1919, the "November revolution" ended in defeat. There remained the "October revolution," which had been imposed upon Germany by the military supremacy of the Allies, and this supremacy was still overwhelming. Even though the revolution of the streets had been defeated, the High Command still needed the republic in order to make peace with the Allies; the Allied armies preserved for the Germans the liberties which they had been unable themselves to defend. In the spring of 1919 the Constituent Assembly met at Weimar, home of Goethe and therefore spiritual centre of German political idealism, but in real life an insignificant little town of no geographic, political, or economic importance, true symbol of German liberalism. The Weimar Assembly was a repetition, almost a parody, of the Frankfort Parliament of 1848. In 1848 the liberals had owed their position, not to their own achievements, but to the breakdown of the old order and revolutionary threat from the masses; yet they had welcomed the defeat of the radicals by the Prussian and Austrian armies and sat in amiable illusion under the protection of Prussian bayonets, until these same beyonets chased them out of existence. In 1919 too the Weimar liberals owed nothing to their own efforts: they were the creation of Allied victory and were themselves protected from radicalism by the Free Corps, the members of which would have liked nothing better than the chance to massacre these liberal idealists. In 1848 the radical menace was broken within a few months; after 1919 the sapping of Allied supremacy was prolonged for a few years. That was the sole difference between the system of Frankfort and the system of Weimar. Or, if there was a further difference, it was that in 1848 the liberals still hoped for success and believed in their own system; in 1919 even the men of Weimar despaired of their ideals. In 1848, with the crumbling of the dynasties, the liberal intellectuals represented all the energies of the middle class; in 1919 the great capitalist middle class was tarred with the "national" disaster, and the intellectuals, impotent and ignored for forty years, were alien to and repudiated by it. By a strange but inevitable paradox, the Weimar

From A. J. P. Taylor, *The Course of German History* (London and New York, 1946), pp. 184–91, 196–97, 202. Reprinted by permission of Hamish Hamilton Ltd., and Coward-McCann, Inc.

constitution was the work of the smallest of the parties in the Assembly, the Democrats; a party without force and almost without backing, but possessing to the full the "spirit of 1848." . . .

The prospect of a peace treaty had almost been forgotten during the constitutional discussions; and so little were the consequences of defeat understood that Hindenburg, moving his headquarters to the east, actually projected a war against the Poles with the aid of the Free Corps, until arrested by an ultimatum from Marshal Foch. Suddenly, at the beginning of May, the Germans were presented with a peace of defeat — admission of responsibility for the war which they had so enthusiastically welcomed; reparations, though not on the scale of Brest-Litovsk; disarmament; and, worst of all, loss of territory to the despised Poles. The discussions of May and June revealed all that was to follow: no German advocated genuine acceptance; the only dispute was whether to reject the treaty at once or to agree to it with the intention of evading, and later undoing, its terms. But to renew the war was impossible: this was the verdict given by the High Command, reluctantly but unmistakably. If Hindenburg had so much as lifted his little finger, war would have blazed out under the restored dictatorship of the High Command; Allied military supremacy forbade it. By their protests the Germans obtained many minor modifications of the original terms; but no modification could remove their essential grievance. For the Treaty of Versailles barred the way against German supremacy in Europe; it confined the Germans to their own national area, compelled them to abandon both Poland and the lands of the Danube, in fact put the Slav peoples of eastern Europe and the Germans on an equality. This was the indelible disgrace. The loss of colonies which had always been an expensive luxury; reparations, which the Germans never supposed they would have to pay; even disarmament, which they knew they could evade — these, perhaps could have been tolerated; but not the suggestion that Poles

and Czechs should rank as "men." The suggestion appeared to Germans so fantastic that even the representatives who signed the treaty made no attempt to conceal their attitude: they were signing so much waste paper, signing solely because the High Command was unable to resume the war. And so, too, the Weimar republic was maintained in being as scapegoat.

The Treaty of Versailles (signed June 28th) gave the final blow to the cause of democracy in Germany, not from any fault of the Allies, but through the blunders and national passion of the Social Democrats. These men, Ebert, Scheidemann, Noske, and the rest, were sincerely democratic: that is, they desired a constitutional state and the rule of law. But they were in awe of "authority" and they shared the national arrogance of every class of German society. Carried to power by no effort of their own, they wished to prove their patriotism — just as the Jacobins had done in France in 1793 and the Bolsheviks in Russia in 1917. But lacking all belief in themselves or conviction in their cause, they took a very different line. Instead of placing the blame for defeat on the old order, instead of guillotining or shooting the Imperial generals and politicians, they helped the old order back into power and bore the burden of its disaster. They would not follow the line of revolutionary war; but still less would they take the line of pacific democratic acceptance. The Social Democrats could claim that, for whatever reason they had opposed Imperial policy before 1914, and that of all parties, except the Independents, they had been most reluctant to support extreme imperialism, while the war was on. It was not their policy which brought Germany to Versailles. But they swallowed without question the view that the liberation of the peoples of eastern Europe was a victory of "entente capitalism." They imagined that the German militarists had become defenders of Socialism; whereas it was the Socialists who had become the advocates of German militarism. Scheidemann, the Social Democrat who had become Chancellor when Ebert was elected President, shouted: "May the hand wither that signs this treaty!" It was the Social Democrats who signed the treaty and their hand which withered. Ludendorff and Hindenburg, the architects of Germany's defeat, became "national" heroes; Ebert lost two sons in the Four Years' War and preserved the Reich in the moment of disaster, but in 1933 his remaining son was martyred in a "national" concentration camp.

The forefront of the "injustice" of Versailles was the severance of Polish territory from the Reich. Most Germans had denied to the Poles any national existence; and even the friends of the Poles had thought only of a Poland carved out of Russia's share of the partitions. All repudiated the loss of the Polish lands. It was a government with Social Democratic members which maintained the separate identity of the remaining fragments of West Prussia and Posen, instead of merging them into the neighbouring provinces, and gave to these fragments the menacing name of *Grenzmark,* the frontier march — clear declaration of impermanency. The Germans could not dispute that the lost lands were inhabited by Poles; but they objected that the wedge of Polish territory ruined East Prussia. In reality the "corridor" was a godsend, for it served to obscure that East Prussia had been equally "ruined" before 1914 and that the cause of its ruin was the existence of the bankrupt Junker estates. Now the maintenance of these estates became a vital obligation of the "national" cause, and, with the approval of all parties, tens of millions of pounds were poured into the bottomless pockets of the Junker landlords, a policy culminating in the gigantic *Osthilfe* of 1927 and that in its turn completing the destruction of the republic. Germans never ceased to rail against the eastern frontier. But, since the lost lands were inhabited by Poles, on what grounds? On the grounds of 1848: the right of the stronger and "healthy national egoism." Thus, the Social Democratic resistance to the Treaty of Versailles inevitably committed them to making Germany once more "the stronger" and so doomed the Weimar republic even before it was born. For the Treaty was signed on June 28th, 1919; the constitution only completed in August. . . .

The republic created by the Constituent Assembly at Weimar lasted in theory for fourteen years, from 1919 to 1933. Its real life was shorter. Its first four years were consumed in the political and economic confusion which followed the Four Years' War; in its last three years there was a temporary dictatorship, half cloaked in legality, which reduced the republic to a sham long before it was openly overthrown. Only for six years did Germany lead a life ostensibly democratic, ostensibly pacific; but in the eyes of many foreign observers these six years appeared as the normal, the "true" Germany, from which the preceding centuries and the subsequent decade of German history were an aberration. A deeper investigation might have found for these six years other causes than the beauty of the German character.

Few Germans, perhaps none, had understood the meaning of the armistice; hardly more took in the meaning of the Treaty of Versailles. For more than four years the Germans had believed that they were winning the war; only for a month (from October 2nd, 1918, until November 11th) were they faced with the truth of defeat, and as soon as the fighting was over the impression of the truth began to fade. The fact of defeat was not yet explained away by the intellectual trick of the "stab in the back," the unfounded allegation of the collapse of the home front; defeat was merely ignored, overlooked. The signing of the treaty was regarded as a gesture of humiliation, brutal but inescapable, which the Allies had imposed upon Germany; but it occurred to no German that the signature would have any consequences. The Germans had not even grasped that, quite apart from the penalties imposed by Versailles, the failure to win the war would compel them to meet at least their own war costs: directly, to deal somehow with the vast national loans by which the war had been exclusively financed; indirectly, to replace the capital equipment which had been worn out during the period of total war. For the Germans, and their sympathizers abroad, never distinguished between the sufferings consequent on defeat and the sufferings consequent on war as such. Germany had fought harder and more completely than any other country; the resultant burden was bound to be greater. Not the Treaty of Versailles, but the delayed strain and exhaustion of four years of military effort produced the economic difficulties of Germany in the post-war years. So little did the Germans grasp this that they blamed the Allies, for instance, for the inadequacy of the German railway services and thought that the victorious Allies ought to reconstruct the railways which had been worn out in conveying German soldiers to the western front.

Thus, immediately after the conclusion of peace, Germans of all classes expected two things: they expected that the Allies, having received their pound of flesh (in the shape of an empty German signature of the Treaty), would now perform out of love for Germany all the services which in other circumstances they would have been compelled to perform by defeat; at the same time the Germans expected to annul, without trouble, the principal enactments of Versailles — enactments which they were sincerely convinced must have been due to some sort of mistake or misunderstanding. In some ways they succeeded almost at once: the trial of war criminals, about which so many promises had been made in Allied countries, turned out the most preposterous farce. The original idea of trial by an international court was soon abandoned — it would be too humiliating for the Germans. Instead the High Court at Leipzig undertook the trials, inflicted a few derisory sentences on non-commissioned officers, gave an even more derisory acquittal to a few generals, until the Allies, become utterly ridiculous, called off the trials altogether. But in other ways the

Germans took things too easily. The Free Corps, veterans of civil slaughter, were moved over to the eastern frontier, where they fought the Poles and maintained the Baltic as a German sphere of influence until well on in 1920. The war against the Poles and the war against German democracy were, as the history of the Free Corps showed, part of the same struggle, the struggle for the restoration of "national" Germany. This connection was obvious to the "national" leaders who arranged the murder of Eisner at one moment and conducted the campaign against the Poles in Upper Silesia the next: it was unfortunately not obvious either to the Allies, who welcomed the defeat of the Independent Socialists, or to the German democrats, who still thought that the "liberation" of Silesia would somehow be also a victory for liberalism in Germany.

* * *

The inflation, more than any other single factor, doomed the republic; its cause was not the policy of the Allies, but the failure to impose direct taxes on the rich.

But inflation had, too, an effect in foreign affairs. To sustain the connection between inflation and reparations, it was necessary to cheat and defy the French and to conduct a steady campaign against Versailles, a campaign which gradually convinced even its authors. Once more Germans began to lose caution and to believe that the war had been won. There was new agitation on the eastern frontiers; open refusal to reduce the German army to the prescribed size; and in the reparations negotiations an insolent, almost jeering, contempt. So long as Versailles could be blamed for all the ills of Germany, no one would demand an account of their stewardship from the old "governing classes" who had brought Germany to this plight and who even now were exploiting her weakness and confusion to consolidate their power. For once, German policy had counted without the French. Poincaré, the

French Prime Minister, actually thought that Versailles ought to be enforced and that the victory of 1918 should be safeguarded. In January 1923, wearied of the refusal to disarm, of the nationalistic agitation, of the failure to pay reparations, Poincaré, backed by the Belgians and Italians, decreed the occupation of the Ruhr, seat of Germany's industrial power. Even now the Germans did not appreciate the position. They still thought there was some mistake, some misunderstanding. Ever since 1870 they had regarded France as decadent and weak, and they could not suppose the French really capable of invading German soil. Moreover, being themselves willing to forget all the abuse and hostility they had directed against England, they supposed, rightly, that this will to forget was reciprocated. Thus, even though the German army could not turn the French out of the Ruhr, the English friends of Germany, anxious to save Germany from "Bolshevism" and chaos, would do it for them. The German government therefore ordered "passive resistance," a great demonstration of national unity against the invader. Factories, mines, banks, offices, in the occupied zone, were everywhere closed. The workers starved in patriotic devotion; the capitalists also suffered in their feelings, though they arranged to sell coal and steel to the French at a high profit. The war, suspended by the armistice of 1918, was renewed.

It was renewed, and lost. The occupation of the Ruhr, far more than the last campaign of 1918, brought home to the Germans the fact of defeat. Until then it had passed unnoticed. Even though fighting had ceased, the Germans had expected the "peril of Bolshevism" to do the trick. Successive German governments had threatened to ruin Germany unless the Treaty of Versailles was torn up. Poincaré called the German bluff: if the Germans wished to ruin Germany rather than acknowledge defeat, they should be allowed to do so. In August 1923, the German industrialists and generals realized that the bluff had not succeeded. Germany had lost the war. A government of fulfilment was formed under Stresemann, leader of the former National Liberals, the "party of the folk." The currency was stabilized, as it could have been stabilized at any moment by a government determined to make revenue and expenditure balance; reparations were paid punctually and without difficulty; even the process of rearmament was temporarily slowed down. The occupation of the Ruhr had been the cold douche which brings a hysteric to her senses. It ended, for the moment, the campaign against Versailles.

* * *

In 1930 the last French troops left the Rhineland and so signed the death-warrant of the Weimar republic. The death of Stresemann, late in 1929, was merely an incident. The victory of the Allied armies had brought the republic to birth; the occupation of the Ruhr had given the republic life; the evacuation of the Rhineland killed it. From start to finish the German republic, and the entire structure of German democracy, owed its existence to the supremacy of Allied arms.

V. WAS THERE REALLY A REVOLUTION?

Improvised Democracy

THEODOR ESCHENBURG

The German November Revolution shattered the formal structure of the Bismarckian Reich. It eliminated the monarchy and monarchical control of the government, it ended the privileged position of the army, it destroyed the legal prerogatives of aristocracy and wealth, and it caused a separation of church and state. Despite this abundance of constitutional change, many observers have questioned how profound the Revolution really was. The German political scientist, Theodor Eschenburg, argues that Germany's democratization was hurriedly improvised to meet urgent foreign and domestic needs. Although not a "democracy without democrats," the Weimar Republic had only a democratic minority, which was forced to fight an uphill battle against an imposing array of surviving authoritarian institutions and social forces. Whether it had a chance of success the student must ultimately decide. Long associated with the liberal-democratic traditions of Southwestern Germany, Eschenburg has been a high civil servant in the Württemberg state government and is now a professor of political science at the University of Tübingen.

HUGO PREUSS, whom Ebert appointed as state secretary of the interior during the provisional government of the People's Commissars and whom he had charged with preparing a draft constitution, published a newspaper article in October 1918 entitled, "The Improvisation of Parliamentarism." Improvisation was the special characteristic of German democracy. Napoleonic France had also transformed itself into a democracy under the impetus of the lost war of 1870–1871, just as tsarist Russia had made a start towards constitutionalism after the unfortunate result of the 1905 war with Japan and overthrew its traditionally autocratic regime as a consequence of defeat in the World War. But in both cases this change was carried out on the basis of a long and intensive intellectual preparation. In Germany only a

small circle of scholars, belonging politically almost without exception to the bourgeois middle class, had concerned itself with the complex questions of a democratic reform of the German state, from a viewpoint partly constitutional, partly also sociological, as in the case of Max Weber. All these works were composed more or less under the influence of the war, out of concern for the inadequacies of current leaders, the sudden turnabout of public opinion, and the uncertain outcome of the war. Their sphere of influence was relatively limited. Theoretical constitutional and sociological works from the viewpoints of Social Democracy and the Center Party were virtually nonexistent. Moderate and independent conservatives like Schmoller and Kaufmann had rejected parliamentarism for various reasons as unsuited for German

From Theodor Eschenburg, *Die improvisierte Demokratie der Weimarer Republik* (Laupheim, 1954), pp. 31–48. Reprinted by permission of Ulrich Steiner-Verlag.

conditions. The Catholic philosopher Max Scheler had come to the same conclusion, although with quite different arguments. And in 1918 Thomas Mann was still denouncing parliamentarism, democracy, and even the reform of the three-class system of voting in Prussia.

All the stronger were the Allied attempts, especially after the entrance of America into the World War, to discredit the monarchy by propaganda, and to win over the Germans for democracy. As long as the German fronts were advancing or at least had suffered no decisive setbacks, this propaganda — partly a means of modern warfare with subversion as its goal, partly an expression of the American and perhaps also English missionary spirit — could only handicap the democratic idea and discredit democratic forces within Germany. This situation changed after the defeat for three reasons: The monarchy had evidently failed; it had promised victory and brought defeat. At first this seemed to prove the justice of the demands of the majority parties for democratic reform and a peace of reconciliation. Allegations about the incapacity and failure of democracy, circulated again and again before and during the war by the right wing, were refuted by the victory of the enemies, since all the Allied powers with the exception of Japan were democratic states. Wilson's demand for the abdication of the Emperor simultaneously made democracy an expiatory sacrifice, a tribute to the allies in expectation of receiving a tolerable peace. One gave up the Bismarckian state structure in order to preserve the Bismarckian state. In the autumn days of 1918 democracy served a function similar to the appointment of Hindenburg in 1916 as commander-in-chief of the army. It awakened in the people the notion of a last resource. This notion, however, also contained an enormous burden. In a tolerable peace treaty, such as Wilson had promised in his fourteen points, German democracy would have received its political legitimation, especially for those broad strata that still thought in Bismarckian and mon-

archist terms and that only moved away from such ideas under the shock of the November events.

But, by the same token, the intolerable — by the standards of the time — Treaty of Versailles produced a widespread and profound disillusionment, above all among the non-socialist elements of the broad middle and lower classes that frequently thought about foreign affairs in the egocentric, kindergarten categories expressed in the motto, "Knowledge of one's own limitations is the first step to improvement." The supporters of democracy were now considered by them either as swindled swindlers or as swindled fools, and democracy as the Trojan horse that one should get rid of as quickly as possible in order to free oneself of the Versailles *Diktat*. Democracy was not the consequence of a domestic effort, the result of a political movement, but was an emergency exit, a tactical expedient; when this expedient, as the peace treaty had showed, did not stand the test, the institution itself was tossed out. The new form of government was deprived of its political legitimation by Versailles.

Democracy in this form was not wanted, it had not been desired. The monarchy was not hated, although the sovereign was exhausted and had to be replaced. But because he was not ready to step down at the right moment, he was overthrown and thus brought the monarchy down with him. He was not overthrown by democratic politicians, however, but by a rebellion of workers and soldiers, radicalized by the stress of war and by Soviet influence, who were concerned primarily with a quick end to the war and only secondarily with the overthrow of the monarchy and — preventing middle-class democracy — the creation of a proletarian dictatorship with the help of foreign intervention. From the point of view of the Weimar constitution the revolution seemed superfluous, for its essentials were already anticipated by the legislation of October 1918, which had been carried out at Ludendorff's behest and bore the signature of the Emperor. Actually the provisional government and the National Assembly, by their quick and determined action, prevented the sovietization of Germany, at least Eastern and Central Germany, which would have meant the division of the Reich, as well as an occupation of the Reich by Allied soldiers, which could have meant dissolution. The preservation of the unity of the Reich, which represented the desire of the entire nation — a sentiment not yet present in 1871 — was the historical service of democracy, primarily of Ebert. It was the real political legitimation of the Weimar Republic. But this complicated course of events in the fall of 1918 was not grasped by wide strata of the population. Demagogic propaganda exploited the situation with a much more primitive version of history: The democrats set up a democracy in Germany only with the help of the enemy democracies and by the path of defeat; they produced this defeat for the sake of their domestic ambitions by means of a conspiracy with the enemy; in a word, they were traitors to their country. Thus arose the stab-in-the-back legend. If Social Democracy stood in fundamental opposition to the Empire, the right now bitterly made war on the new state. It was antidemocratic. Its great propaganda weapon was the battle against the "Versailles *Diktat*," which was now solely blamed for all misfortune, all distress; the right put forth its political ballyhoo at such a volume as to drown out every successful revision of every government. No German politician — not even on the right — could have attained more than was attained — it knew that. But by this propagandistic outbidding it fought the Republic most effectively, debilitating it most promisingly. Certainly even with an incomparably milder peace treaty, a restoration party would have come into being, a fascist organization might have developed. The decisions of the peace conference of Versailles, however, gave these movements their impetus, the breadth of their effectiveness. This propaganda had such a strong resonance because wide strata, far beyond the right, were inwardly bound

to the authoritarian state and looked upon the democratic state with skepticism if not antipathy. Their state was a father, now they were all the state; that they could not and did not want to grasp. They were not able to assimilate in heart and mind this improvised changeover from an authoritarian to a participatory state. They longed for the traditional authoritarian and bureaucratic government.

The result of this improvisation, however, was that democratization, and particularly its participatory element, was not carried out systematically. This improvisation prevented the democratic parties from recognizing in time the significance of the positions of the counter-revolutionaries, from seeing them for what they were and disposing of them. It was improvisation that endangered the systematic strengthening and securing of the new state form. Thus democracy bogged down from the outset; the new ruling parties, above all Social Democracy and the Center, wanted to take over the power of the fallen authoritarian state. The old dynastic division of *Länder* was retained, and nothing was done, especially in Prussia, except for the general introduction of the democratic franchise, to promote the expansion and development of self-government in the provinces, districts, and communities.

The decisive point, however, is this: because democracy was mortgaged by the terms of the Versailles Treaty, if not solely for this reason, a number of feudal and authoritarian institutions — especially those directly or indirectly affected by these terms — were able to escape every attempt at democratic adaptation and were able to preserve or restore their unassailable position of predominance and privilege. They derived from these paragraphs of the Versailles *Diktat* a new political legitimation for their preservation and privileged position. To put it very explicitly, even rebellious acts [*Hochverrat*], directed against the Versailles Treaty, could claim the protection of the treason [*Landesverrat*] law.

The German armed forces were limited

to 100,000 men according to the Versailles Treaty. They could not have at their disposal heavy artillery, tanks, airplanes, submarines, or dreadnoughts; and they had to dissolve the general staff. The introduction of general conscription or a militia system was forbidden. An Allied control commission was instituted for the purpose of supervision. As a result of this numerical restriction, in order to compensate with the highest possible quality, officer and noncommissioned officer positions were filled with the most competent and experienced men; such men, however, could only come from the old army and navy. Concern to prevent a repetition of the Prussian "Krümper system" that followed the Treaty of Tilsit made the replacement of discharged servicemen possible only to a very limited extent, and the German armed forces rightly undertook the selection of recruits with special care in order to create an élite army. This selection, however, lay in the hands of the old officers, who took into account not only military efficiency and the necessary homogeneity but also political attitudes, since they selected men with a background and social standing similar to their own and rejected all others. In personnel structure there arose thus a miniature edition of the imperial armed forces. The fact that soldiers and officers were not allowed to be politically active was an understandable measure, which existed also in other democracies. In the latter, however, it operated as a passing restraint merely for the period of service, while in Germany it was an obligation binding for 12 to 25 years. In this vacuum, created by a justified neutralization, there was consciously introduced a tradition of the old army (which had been cultivated in the interest of increasing military performance) of deliberately cutting the armed forces off from the rest of the political world. Not only was a strong homogeneity of attitude thereby attained, but also an anti-democratic orientation. Thus came into being a monarchistic island of Prussian-feudal observance, even if loosened up

and reformed, whose commander under Ebert was at first the chief of the army command, General von Seeckt, and after Seeckt's dismissal in 1926, Reich President von Hindenburg, in whom the armed forces now found once again a genuine supreme warlord, a substitute Kaiser. The technical and numerical limitations together with the Allied control soon pressed the armed forces into illegality. In this position, imposed by the enemy, the distinction between the external dealings forbidden by the peace treaty and the internal dealings forbidden by the constitution quickly and easily disappeared, especially since the two overlapped. Under the pressure of the treaty stipulations, any revelation of the armed forces' illegality was regarded as treason, and most such revelations were suppressed by means of the treason law. Thus emerged in the Weimar Republic an almost completely autonomous military power, incompatible with democracy, constructed on monarchist principles, which evaded democratic control under the protection of national defense and of necessary illegality. It had a secret right of veto which could be of decisive significance in cases of conflict. The Reichswehr was not simply an instrument in the hands of the counter-revolutionaries, but neither was it an absolutely dependable republican institution. Simply by its existence, thanks to the conservative attitude of its leadership, it exercised a protective function over institutions handed down from the monarchy and incompatible with democracy. It sought in this way to create a protective sphere for the preservation of its own existence. To a certain extent it carried out active policies, though very carefully and secretly; for example, the first negotiations with the Soviet Union leading to the Rappallo Treaty in 1922 were initiated by the defense ministry, not by the foreign office.

The experiences of the World War showed the great significance in wartime of armaments and basic industry, as well as agriculture. From these considerations, further strengthened by the interests and economic biases of officers who came predominantly from circles connected with the great estates and — to a certain extent — with heavy industry, the Reichswehr was strongly interested that nothing change with respect to private enterprise in industry and agriculture. There was not only the worry that production might decline in any restructuring such as the socialization of large-scale enterprises and the division or expropriation of large estates, but even more — since steel and light metal production, the arms industry, ship-building, and parts of the chemical industry had quickly been drawn into the Reichswehr's realm of illegal activity — there was the concern to prevent from the outset any kind of control by institutions such as the trade unions, which were independent of the firm, and politically involved. Heavy industry and large landed property had been the two great feudal stewards of the Empire. They retained this predominant position to a surprising extent in the Weimar Republic. They were simultaneously the strongest opponents and the exploiters of the Republic. Not only for military — as little as these are to be underestimated — but also for other reasons the Versailles Treaty functioned as the protector of the two great economic powers. The socialization of heavy industry was shied away from because of the fear that nationalization would give the French, whose drive to the Ruhr was already then apparent, a formal right, according to the legal views of the time, to confiscation as a replacement or as a pledge for unpaid reparations. No one wanted to create a political disturbance in the occupied areas and their vicinity by an action which could possibly push the employers concerned over to the side of the occupying power, France, especially since inadequate parliamentary support made it impossible yet to think at all of socialization. One shrank from such an experiment in the midst of the postwar crisis, one feared that such an intervention would worsen the German position with the capitalist Allied powers, especially America, whose credits

were already hoped for. All non-socialist parties, even the Center, in which the working class gained more and more influence after the Revolution, were opponents of any kind of socialization, because in such action, even if restricted to heavy industry, they saw a precedent and feared its extension to other branches of the economy. Even small businessmen, thanks to very intensive and widespread propaganda, became the loyal supporters of heavy industry.

For the same reasons there was a timidity about agrarian reform. To be sure, peasant resettlement in the East was repeatedly demanded by the socialist program as well as by democratic groups; to be sure Article 155 of the Weimar constitution prescribed the dissolution of entailed estates in order to set up the preconditions for a proper redistribution of large estates; to be sure a Reich settlement law had been enacted for this purpose in August 1919; but not only was money unavailable, above all political initiative and activity were lacking. There were only two possibilities in the East: namely, direct subvention and high protective tariffs on the one hand, or land redistribution and expropriation on the other. The latter alternative was feared. East Prussia was separated from the Reich by the Corridor, West Prussia and Silesia were amputated, and Pomerania and Brandenburg had become border provinces. In this situation, changed as a consequence of the peace treaty, the great estate owners, like the Reichswehr, found their position elevated indirectly through the incursions of the enemy. If for almost two centuries they had enjoyed a privileged position in the monarchy thanks to royal grace, now they retained it as defenders of the borderland thanks to national defense needs. To be sure the estate jurisdictions which permitted most of the landowners to exert public legal force over their employees were abolished, if only in 1927; to be sure agricultural workers' unions developed their activity intensively and comprehensively after the Revolution; but nothing essential changed in the social structure of the East.

The Reichsland Federation, in which the East Elbian landowners set the tone, knew how to secure the support of the peasants, even the South German peasant organizations, whose needs because of their processing interests were quite different from those of the Eastern landowners. In the minds of a wide segment of the people, the iron and steel industry and the Eastern estates were not simply branches of the economy but national institutions whose interests were tabu; the democratic Republic could not break the power of myth which lay in the name Krupp, "the armament smithy of the Reich," and in the old Prussian nobility, whose names children often learned in school. In the Reichswehr, in the great estates, and in heavy industry, then, those elements remained which, thanks to tradition or assimilation, knew how to govern and were more than a match for the new rulers, the honorable but insecure petty bourgeois, or the academicians still trapped in the old authoritarian and feudal way of thinking. It is an astounding phenomenon that, despite the collapse of the dynasty, despite the elimination of the three-class system of voting, despite the dissolution of the Prussian House of Lords, nonetheless the East Elbian estate owners retained their predominant position in the democratic Republic. This can only be explained by the attitude and influence of the armed forces, the predilections and apprehensions of the bourgeois parties respecting private property (perhaps with the exception of a part of the Democrats), and the nationally elevated position of the great estates that stemmed from the peace treaty.

The survival of these three imperial power factors in the Republic had a crucial influence on the development of German democracy. The second Reich president, von Hindenburg, who was elected in 1925, had been the last head of the old army and was, to the bottom of his heart, a Junker. That a representative of the armed forces and the East Elbian estates was head of state strengthened the power of both in politics, as well as that of heavy industry

because of their close connections, and all the more so because the Reich president by the constitution exercised very extensive and drastic powers. He was supreme commander of the armed forces, he could engage these forces against a rebellious *Land*, he could declare a state of siege and transfer executive power to the Reichswehr. To be sure the Reichstag could nullify these measures, but the Reich president was always at least one jump ahead of parliament because he had the right of practical execution. The Reich president could dismiss the chancellor and the ministers as well as officials and military officers without consulting parliament or the government; without his approval, however, none of these could be appointed. He could in certain cases dissolve parliament. To be sure, for all of these measures, even those of a military character, he needed the countersignature of the chancellor or a minister, but since he exercised the right of dismissal, he had almost a free hand in cases of conflict.

In constitutional literature, as in the debates of the Weimar National Assembly, the institution of the Reich presidency has been represented as a compromise between the French and American presidencies. That may be right. The decisive model, however, was the constitutional position of the German emperor. The bourgeois parties were still too dominated by authoritarian thinking, too distrustful of their own ability to govern, to be able to dispense with a substitute Kaiser. They believed it impossible to do without a dictator on call in cases of emergency and conflict, for a *deus ex machina* in case parliament — i.e., they themselves — should fail. The Reich president is much more of a compromise figure between monarchical constitutionalism and democratic parliamentarism than between the American and French constitutions. It was indeed a monarchical element in the Republic but an indispensable one in view of the improvisation of democracy and the domestic and international situation of the Reich. The great tragedy of German democracy was the early death of Ebert and the election of an old Prussian general as his successor. By this arrangement that old constitutional dualism between the head of state and the parliament, which Robert von Mohl had already warned against, was continued into the democratic era, even if in a diluted form. In the debates of the Weimar National Assembly the Social Democrats resolutely opposed a powerful presidency, but all the more strongly did Ebert, who had been elected provisional Reich president in February 1919, strive to create one, in cooperation with the bourgeois parties. After he was unsuccessful in saving the monarchy he wanted at least to preserve part of this institution in the Republic. The constitutional stipulations concerning the head of state seemed ideally tailored for Ebert, who was held in high esteem by the bourgeois parties because of his independence from the parties, his self-assurance, and his integrity. Anxiety about domestic unrest and external pressure, about the disintegration of the Reich through regional separatism in the East and West, through Communist uprisings, or through Allied intervention, all helped to induce the majority to provide the Reich with the strongest possible head of state.

In order to counter as much as possible the spread of disturbances produced by the lost war and the Revolution, Ebert had the greatest interest in keeping the old administration intact and, for this purpose, keeping the old officials in office. This transition was carried out more easily because the Emperor and the German princes had released all officials and military officers from their oaths, in order that they might continue their service under the new regime without internal conflict. Hindenburg served as their model when he remained commander-in-chief of the army after, and in spite of, the abdication of the Emperor. The creation of the People's Commissars, as well as the workers' and soldiers' councils, merely established a political superstructure over the old monarchical administrative apparatus, which continued to operate essentially undisturbed. The majority of the Center Party and the Democrats had, to be sure, come over to the democratic republic under the pressure of circumstances, but they wanted to see as little as possible changed in the substructure of the state. In the leftward shift of the November Revolution these two parties moved to the right. They assumed vis-à-vis Social Democracy some of the functions of the political right, the real right holding back completely at first, in the shock of the monarchy's collapse, until the announcement of the peace treaty.

In order to secure the personnel for this administration, officials were guaranteed "their duly acquired rights." Corresponding to the spirit of the new democracy officials were also granted freedom in their political convictions and free expression of opinion. The simultaneous guarantee of duly acquired rights and freedom of political conviction, a highly paradoxical regulation if one thinks of those old monarchical officials, was to prove itself very non-functional in practice. This guarantee of duly acquired rights experienced a certain restriction in 1922 when by law the circle of political officials who could be temporarily pensioned off was considerably expanded. Simultaneously, as a reaction to counterrevolutionary activity in the Kapp Putsch as well as to the assassination of Erzberger and Rathenau, the Weimar parties exerted a strong pressure to fill official positions with republicans, thus with their own supporters, who were largely excluded from the state administration under the monarchy. At first a unique situation existed — and had after-effects down to 1933 — in which the top positions were democratized while the entire substructure, thanks to its composition, retained an authoritarian character. This inherited bureaucracy was not — with exceptions — expressly counter-revolutionary but it was on the whole nondemocratic. It still thought and worked in authoritarian categories. It tried to preserve an administrative state. In its conception, the monarchical authoritarian state had been transformed into a republican authoritarian state. In time a series of higher positions in the ministries, leading positions in the district and lower administration such as heads of government and police, as well as rural magistrates, were occupied by members of the republican parties, and even partially by outsiders. But that did not change the essential character of this authoritarian bureacracy, which considered itself to be the true nucleus of the state behind the vicissitudes of governmental coalitions. Basically the high quality of administration was more important to the population than the political attitude of the officialdom.

Also the irremovability of judges was maintained in the Republic, which took over without restriction the judges of the monarchy. In the Third Republic France abolished irremovability for a short period by means of a constitutional law in order to achieve a republicanization of the judiciary. The old German judge was still mentally living in imperial times, and this manifested itself frequently in his attitude during trial proceedings and in his judgments. A large number of judges made grave errors and blunders in their utterances and in their decisions, especially in political trials — e.g., libel of the Reich president and Reich chancellor, insult to the new Reich colors, black-red-gold, and to the Republic, as well as in the sentencing of counter-revolutionaries — which can only be explained by this judicial bias entailed from former times. Such a respected and independent jurist as Gustav Radbruch, then Reich minister of justice, spoke of a "state of war between the nation and the judicial system." Although the Social Democrats, partially supported by several Democrats, very emphatically demanded the temporary repeal of the irremovability of judges, such action was rejected.

Crucial in the decision to retain officials and judges was the desire to end the revolution as quickly as possible, and the feeling that this bias against democracy was a temporary phenomenon, which would diminish from year to year and gradually dis-

appear with the occupation of these positions by a generation brought up under democracy.

Also at the German universities, instructors — albeit nominated by the senates or faculties but appointed by the monarch — lectured on in the same manner as they had during the Empire, sometimes even more radically, in a more stridently monarchist and anti-democratic fashion. They likewise enjoyed the status of public officials for whom the guarantee of duly acquired rights pertained. On top of this came the special protection of academic freedom and the autonomy of educational institutions which the Republic preserved most painstakingly. The consequence was that college students were frequently taught undemocratic, in part strongly anti-democratic, values. The student corporations, with their monarchist traditions and nationalist resentments, with their outdated aristocratic social attitudes, still frequently exerted through their alumni organizations a significant influence on the filling of official positions. To intervene against such things would violate the legal protection of personal freedom. To be sure a number of serious and committed democratic instructors taught at the institutions of higher education. Their circle expanded gradually, as did the number of democratically minded students. But the romantically inclined circles of instructors and students who played around with the idea of restoration or counter-revolution constituted a strong element at these institutions. They used their influence, in part unconsciously, in part deliberately, to keep alive the old anti-democratic values and pass them on to the new generation.

In contrast to the Catholic Church, which expressly accepted all forms of government so long as they met ecclesiastical requirements, the German Lutheran Church was most intimately connected with the monarchical form of government, for the reason that the sovereign was also the *summus episcopus*. Especially in Northern and Eastern Germany it was a decidedly monarchist-conservative institution. In the countryside a close relationship existed between the clergy and great estate owners. The liberal-democratic tendency was considered and treated as completely alien by the preponderant majority. They greeted democracy not as liberation from authoritarian tutelage, but as an institution foreign to them and their church, to which they felt as opposed as they felt tied to the old princely authority. But with the collapse of the monarchy large circles of Lutheran Protestants lost their political orientation and support; they became politically homeless. The more evident it became in the second half of the twenties that there was no prospect of a restoration, the more widespread and profound became the process of disintegration on the part of the Protestant parties, while the Center Party and also the Social Democrats preserved their solidarity and popular support through all the elections down to 1933.

These two, combined with the shrinking Democratic Party, formed the democratic-republican bloc in parliament. It was called the Weimar Coalition. Its symbol was the newly created black-red-gold flag. Opposite it stood the anti-democratic bloc, which was composed of the Nationalists, the supporters of the German People's Party — the Reichstag fraction of the German People's Party, by contrast, pursued a clear republican policy as long as Stresemann was in the government (1925–1929), thanks to his firm and strong leadership, only to slide back immediately after his death into the anti-democratic camp — as well as the gradually developing middle-class splinter parties, and finally the National Socialists, who became in the election of 1930 the second largest, and 1932 the largest, party in the Reichstag. They formed, despite all conflicts, the black-white-red front, and were opponents of parliamentary democracy and supporters of an authoritarian system of government, a restoration or dictatorship. To the anti-democratic group also belonged their bitterest opponents, the Communists.

Between the authoritarian and feudal elements on one hand and the groups of the black-white-red front on the other there existed an abundance of more or less visible relationships differing by very gradual degrees in their intensity. They protected, supported, and strengthened each other in diverse ways. All nuances could be found, from open resistance to a quiet longing for restoration and the old, well-ordered authoritarian state, from anxiety about private property and fear of socialism (which was considered by many to be merely a modified form of Communism) to authoritarian and imperialistic speculations on a Führer and a power state [*Machtstaat*]. The presidential election of 1925 saw a first test of strength in the conflict between the two groups. It was equivalent to the election of an emperor by the people; it was a plebiscite for the old authoritarian state. When this "substitute emperor" did not show himself willing to carry out the anti-democratic wishes of his supporters, they voted against him in 1932 and for Hitler. To prevent his election, the Republicans now voted for Hindenburg. By the elections of 1932 the German nation was split "into four main blocs, which stood for four incompatible forms of government — communism, fascism, democracy, and constitutional-authoritarian monarchy." The aristocratic current, which occupied the traditional, authoritarian, feudal institutions and whose political representatives were in the German National and German People's parties, thought to avail themselves at the proper moment of the plebian current, whose *avant-garde* was National Socialism, for the purpose of restoration, and therefore strengthened it to such an extent as to become its eventual victim. It thought to lead and found itself led. This "plebian conservatism," called up and organized in the mid-seventies by the feudal element in order to provide voting support after the introduction of general suffrage for the Reichstag, could be harnessed and controlled by the authoritarian state down to 1918. In the Republic, however, it emancipated itself from the old ruling stratum to go its own way and strive for its own goals. Nevertheless, among the National Socialists there were countless numbers who hoped Hitler would restore domestically and internationally the Bismarckian Reich. The Weimar Republic was not a democracy without democrats, but a democracy with a democratic minority. "In the domestic two-front war the best efforts of the democracy were consumed." To be sure, the indecision of Wilhelm II aggravated the introduction of democracy, the peace treaty imposed a heavy burden upon it; to be sure the economic crises following the war undermined the credit of democracy just as economic prosperity had added to the credit of the Empire. The vital point, however, remains the improvised establishment of a participatory state organization at a time when the nation was still bound to an authoritarian tradition.

The "above-party" state, which the Empire had never really been but seemed to be for many, especially in memory, the justly ruled and well-administered state, about which one did not have to concern himself particularly, remained even after the experiences of the World War a genuine political ideal for numberless Germans. They did not, to be sure, know how they were to realize it and waited for someone who would realize it for them. Within 14 years Germany had recovered astonishingly from the tremendously heavy blow of the Versailles *Diktat*, it had at the very end mastered the great economic crisis, but it was not able to overcome the collapse of the monarchical administrative state.

SUGGESTIONS FOR ADDITIONAL READING

There is now an ample literature on the creation of the Weimar Republic and scholarship is especially active at the present time. The reader may want to begin with a broader perspective on German history and culture. He is already acquainted with three writers whose general surveys are of more than usual interest: Koppel S. Pinson, Golo Mann, and A. J. P. Taylor. More extensive is the three-volume work of Hajo Holborn, *A History of Germany* (New York, 1959–   ), of which the final volume, dealing with the period since 1840, has not yet appeared. On the much disputed subject of German national character, it is best to read both the sharply critical work of Louis L. Snyder, *German Nationalism, Tragedy of a People* (Harrisburg, 1952) and the more sympathetic analysis of Robert H. Lowie, *Toward Understanding Germany* (Chicago, 1954).

The general history of the German November Revolution and the Weimar Republic is still best approached by the English-reading student in the classic volume of S. William Halperin, from which a selection was drawn. A survey of other works on this period of German history may proceed from right to left according to the political sympathies of the author. One may sample the Nazi interpretation in E. Anrich, *Deutsche Geschichte von 1918–1939* (Leipzig and Berlin, 1940). The best conservative-nationalist account is Erich Volkmann, *Revolution über Deutschland* (Oldenburg, 1930); also see Alfred Niemann, *Revolution von oben – Umsturz von unten* (Berlin, 1927). An important recent assessment of the republican years by a moderate conservative is Karl Dietrich Erdmann, "Die Geschichte der Weimarer Republik als Problem der Wissenschaft," *Vierteljahrshefte für Zeitgeschichte*, III (1955), 1–19; it was this assessment that inspired Peter von Oertzen's Third Way rebuttal reprinted above.

In the liberal camp, the reader is already familiar with two leading writers, Friedrich Meinecke and Theodor Eschenburg. Another classic is Ferdinand Friedensburg, *Die Weimarer Republik*, 2nd ed. (Hannover and Frankfurt/Main, 1957). More extensive but somewhat disappointing is the two-volume work of Erich Eyck, *A History of the Weimar Republic*, trans. Harlan P. Hanson and Robert G. L. Waite (Cambridge, Mass., 1963–1964). Two leading Social Democrats may represent their party's interpretation: Eduard Bernstein, *Die deutsche Revolution* (Berlin, 1921), and Friedrich Stampfer, *Die vierzehn Jahre der ersten deutschen Republik*, 3rd ed. (Hamburg, 1953). Of course Hermann Müller's memoir-history, quoted above, belongs to this group as well.

Somewhere between the Social Democrats and the Communists lies the important writing of Arthur Rosenberg. *A History of the German Republic*, from which the extract above was reprinted, forms part of a two-volume set, of which the first — and perhaps more important — volume is titled, *The Birth of the German Republic*, trans. Ian F. D. Morrow (London, 1931). It has recently been reprinted in a paperbound edition under the title, *Imperial Germany* (Boston, 1964). Similar in approach is the early history of the USPD spokesman, Heinrich Ströbel, *The German Revolution and After*, trans. H. J. Stenning (New York, 1923), as is the interesting but anecdotal and undocumented volume of Rudolf Coper, *Failure of a Revolution* (Cambridge, Mass., 1955). The official Communist historiography of the Revolution begins with the *Illustrierte Geschichte der Deutschen Revolution* (Berlin, 1929). For recent East German Communist views, one should see their principal historical journal, *Zeitschrift für Geschichtswissenschaft*, especially Volume VI (1958) for articles written during the fortieth anniversary year of the Revolution. Here one may find recent reinterpretations, such as that of

Roland Bauer, as well as older Stalinist assessments like that of Walter Nimtz, "Über den Charakter der Novemberrevolution von 1918/1919 in Deutschland," VI (1958), 687–715.

A survey of diverse viewpoints would not be complete without a sampling of Germanophobic writings. Bitterly hostile are W. M. Knight-Patterson, *Germany from Defeat to Conquest* (London, 1945) and Godfrey Scheele, *The Weimar Republic, Overture to the Third Reich* (London, 1946). Somewhat more scholarly is the work of the French historian Edmond Vermeil, published in an English abridgement, *Germany in the Twentieth Century* (New York, 1956).

The editor's own views on the Revolution are developed in Richard N. Hunt, "Friedrich Ebert and the German Revolution of 1918," *The Responsibility of Power*, Leonard Krieger and Fritz Stern, eds. (New York, 1967), pp. 315–334.

To proceed to more detailed studies of special topics, one may approach the domestic political history of wartime Germany in the first Rosenberg volume, cited above. Other special studies include Albrecht Mendelssohn-Bartholdy, *The War and German Society* (New Haven, 1937); Gerald D. Feldman, *Army, Industry, and Labor in Germany, 1914–1918* (Princeton, 1966); and Reinhard Patemann, *Der Kampf um die preussische Wahlreform im Ersten Weltkrieg* (Düsseldorf, 1964).

In his review article reprinted above, Klaus Epstein deals with three important works on the history of the crucial Social Democratic Party: Peter Gay, *The Dilemma of Democratic Socialism, Eduard Bernstein's Challenge to Marx* (New York, 1952); Carl E. Schorske, *German Social Democracy, 1905–1917* (Cambridge, Mass., 1955); and A. Joseph Berlau, *The German Social Democratic Party, 1914–1921* (New York, 1949). More sympathetic to the SPD are the relevant chapters of Carl Landauer's excellent *European Socialism* (2 vols., Berkeley and Los Angeles, 1959). For Social Democratic attitudes toward na-

tionalism, see Hermann Heidegger, *Die deutsche Sozialdemokratie und der nationale Staat, 1870–1920* (Göttingen, 1956); for their relations with the trade unions, Heinz Josef Varain, *Freie Gewerkschaften, Sozialdemokratie und Staat* (Düsseldorf, 1956); and for internal party development, Richard N. Hunt, *German Social Democracy, 1918–1933* (New Haven and London, 1964). There is no adequate history of the USPD, but Eugen Prager's outdated *Geschichte der USPD* (Berlin, 1921) still has some utility.

The history of German Communism is treated in Ossip K. Flechtheim, *Die Kommunistische Partei Deutschlands in der Weimarer Republik* (Offenbach/Main, 1948). On special topics there is of course Eric Waldman's study of the Spartacist uprising; also Richard A. Comfort, *Revolutionary Hamburg* (Stanford, 1966); Werner T. Angress, *Stillborn Revolution, The Communist Bid for Power in Germany, 1921–1923* (Princeton, 1963); and the memoir-history of Ruth Fischer, *Stalin and German Communism* (Cambridge, Mass., 1948).

Other important studies of German parties which deal with the Revolutionary period include: Rudolf Morsey, *Die Deutsche Zentrumspartei, 1917–1923* (Düsseldorf, 1966); Henry Ashby Turner, Jr., *Stresemann and the Politics of the Weimar Republic* (Princeton, 1963); and Werner Liebe, *Die Deutschnationale Volkspartei, 1919–1924* (Düsseldorf, 1956). The standard work on German parties is Ludwig Bergsträsser, *Geschichte der politischen Parteien in Deutschland,* 10th ed. (Munich, 1960); also see Sigmund Neumann, *Die deutschen Parteien* (Berlin, 1932).

To study military questions one may begin with John W. Wheeler-Bennett's masterpiece, *The Nemesis of Power, The German Army in Politics, 1918–1945* (London, 1953), now supplemented by another excellent British critique, F. L. Carsten, *The Reichswehr and Politics, 1918–1933* (London, 1966). Robert G. L. Waite, *Vanguard of Nazism* (Cambridge, Mass.,

1952) is a first-rate study of the *Freikorps*. More sympathetic to the German military is Harold J. Gordon, Jr., *The Reichswehr and the German Republic, 1919–1926* (Princeton, 1957). With respect to other surviving imperial institutions, there have been two recent German studies of the bureaucracy: Wolfgang Elben, *Das Problem der Kontinuität in der deutschen Revolution* (Düsseldorf, 1965); and Wolfgang Runge, *Politik und Beamtentum im Parteienstaat* (Stuttgart, 1965). There is still no adequate volume on the Weimar judiciary, but one may refer to Ernst Fraenkel, *Zur Soziologie der Klassenjustiz* (Berlin, 1927). On monarchist activities, see Walter H. Kaufmann, *Monarchism in the Weimar Republic* (New York, 1953).

After long neglect the council movement has recently received scholarly attention in three excellent German studies. The first is the full-length work of the author whose article was reprinted above: Peter von Oertzen, *Betriebsräte in der Novemberrevolution* (Düsseldorf, 1963); also see Eberhard Kolb, *Die Arbeiterräte in der deutschen Innenpolitik, 1918–1919* (Düsseldorf, 1962); and the somewhat older Walter Tormin, *Zwischen Rätediktatur und sozialer Demokratie* (Düsseldorf, 1954).

The unique course of the Revolution in Bavaria has special interest: one may compare the Bavarian interpretation of Karl Schwend, *Bayern zwischen Monarchie und Diktatur* (Munich, 1954), with the East German version of Hans Beyer, *Von der Novemberrevolution zur Räterepublik in München* (Berlin, 1957). The most recent assessment of these events is by an American: Allan Mitchell, *Revolution in Bavaria, 1918–1919* (Princeton, 1965). The standard history of the Weimar constitution is Willibald Apelt, *Geschichte der Weimarer Verfassung* (Munich, 1946).

On the Treaty of Versailles, one may begin with A. Luckau, *The German Delegation at the Paris Peace Conference* (New York, 1941). For the economic effects of the treaty on Germany there is the classic debate between John Maynard Keynes, *The Economic Consequences of the Peace* (London, 1919), and Etienne Mantoux, *The Carthaginian Peace* (Oxford, 1946). Also see Karl Bergmann, *The History of Reparations* (Boston, 1927), and Karsten Laursen and Jørgen Pedersen, *The German Inflation, 1918–1923* (Amsterdam, 1964). John H. Morgan, *Assize of Arms* (London, 1945) is the standard treatment of Germany's disarmament and rearmament.

For individuals prominent in the Revolutionary period there is a dearth of good biographies. One may consult Waldemar Besson, *Friedrich Ebert, Verdienst und Grenze* (Göttingen, 1963), and Klaus Epstein, *Matthias Erzberger and the Dilemma of German Democracy* (Princeton, 1959), which are exceptions to the rule. Memoirs and memoir material are more abundant and may be found for the following figures: William II, Prince Max of Baden, Wilhelm Groener, Friedrich Ebert, Philipp Scheidemann, Gustav Noske, Otto Meissner, Emil Barth, Richard Müller, Otto Braun, and Carl Severing.

Of the many documentary collections, one of the most valuable for our purposes has recently been published: Charles B. Burdick and Ralph H. Lutz (eds.), *The Political Institutions of the German Revolution* (New York, 1966). It contains in English translation the minutes of the following governmental bodies: Prince Max's cabinet, the Council of People's Commissars, the Executive Council, the First National Congress of Councils, the Central Council, and the Scheidemann cabinet. This may be used in combination with Lutz' older collection of Revolutionary documents, *The Fall of the German Empire* (2 vols., Stanford, 1932). German documentation begins with the monumental result of the Reichstag's Committee of Inquiry, *Die Ursachen des deutschen Zusammenbruchs im Jahre 1918* (12 vols., Berlin, 1928), from which Lutz has compiled a volume of extracts in English, *Causes of the German Collapse* (Stanford, 1934). More recently the Kommission für Geschichte des Parlamentarismus und der politischen Parteien has supplemented this material with Erich Matthias (ed.), *Der Interfraktionelle Ausschuss, 1917/18* (Düsseldorf, 1959); and Erich Matthias and Rudolf Morsey (eds.), *Die Regierung des Prinzen Max von Baden* (Düsseldorf, 1962). For the official minutes of the National Assembly, see *Verhandlungen der verfassunggebenden deutschen Nationalversammlung* (8 vols., Berlin, 1919–1920). An East German collection of documents has been published by their Institut für Marxismus-Leninismus, *Die Novemberrevolution in Deutschland, Dokumente und Materialen* (Berlin, 1958).

Several bibliographical articles have appeared recently which contain not only reviews of historical literature but often important interpretative insights. Perhaps the best is Eric C. Kollman, "Reinterpreting Modern German History: The Weimar Republic," *Journal of Central European Affairs*, XXI (1962), 434–451. Also see: Erich Matthias, "Zur Geschichte der Weimarer Republik," *Die Neue Gesellschaft*, VIII (1956), 312–320; and Thilo Vogelsang, "Neuere Literatur zur Geschichte der Weimarer Republik," *Vierteljahrshefte für Zeitgeschichte*, IX (1961), 211–224. To keep up to date with new publications, the interested reader should follow the extensive bibliographies published in the *Vierteljahrshefte für Zeitgeschichte*.